BROKEN

Redeeming the life you were meant to live.

BRIANT CUFFY

FREILING
AGENCY

Bible versions used:

English Standard Version (ESV)
The Holy Bible, English Standard Version. ESV® Text Edition: 2016.
Copyright © 2001 by Crossway Bibles, a publishing ministry of
Good News Publishers.

New American Standard Bible (NASB)
New American Standard Bible®, Copyright © 1960, 1971, 1977,
1995, 2020 by The Lockman Foundation. All rights reserved.

New International Version (NIV)
Holy Bible, New International Version®, NIV® Copyright ©1973,
1978, 1984, 2011 by Biblica, Inc.® Used by permission.
All rights reserved worldwide.

New King James Version (NKJV)
Scripture taken from the New King James Version®.
Copyright © 1982 by Thomas Nelson. Used by permission.
All rights reserved.

King James Version (KJV). Public Domain

The Message (MSG). Copyright © 1993, 2002, 2018
by Eugene H. Peterson

Published by Freiling Agency, LLC.

P.O. Box 1264
Warrenton, VA 20188

www.FreilingAgency.com

PB ISBN: 979-8-9881634-8-0
eBook ISBN: 979-8-9881634-9-7

Printed in the United States of America

Dedication

*To my wife Carrie, in whose resilient love this
broken heart has found a home.*

Contents

Foreword

by Mark Benson

In a world often consumed by the noise of progress and the relentless pursuit of success, it is a rare gift to encounter a voice that speaks to the quiet truths that shape our souls. Such a voice can be found in the gentle wisdom and profound insights of Briant Cuffy, a man whose presence in my life has been nothing short of transformative.

I first met Briant on Labor Day 2011 as part of a search process for the Pastor of Adult Ministries at First Baptist Church in Minneapolis, Minnesota. In those early days, our connection was a simple thread spun by the search for a pastor, an office, and a role to be filled. Yet, over the course of the past twelve years, that thread has woven a tapestry of friendship, love, and understanding that has stretched beyond the confines of titles and positions and transcended the ordinary boundaries of time and location. Through countless conversations, shared experiences, and heartfelt prayers, I have witnessed Briant's evolution—not just as a person, but as a seeker, a believer, and a servant of Christ.

Our paths converged not by chance, but through a joy-filled friendship that was clearly guided by a greater hand. As a product development consultant, a high-tech executive, and author of a book on thermo-dynamics (*The Art of Software Thermal Management for Embedded Systems, Springer 2014*), my professional world was characterized by algorithms and systems, by logic and precision. But it was through the unas-suming vessel of Briant's friendship that I was led to explore a different realm—one of faith, introspection, and the profound questions that lie beneath the surface of human existence.

Briant and I, two men from different backgrounds, found common ground in our shared yearning for belonging and love. As we shared our own experiences, exploring the echoes of our relationships with our earthly fathers and the impact of those connections on our souls, we simultaneously journeyed towards a deeper understanding of our heavenly Father's bound-less love. It was through these conversations that Briant guided me toward a truth I had long known in my mind but had struggled to embrace in my heart: that I, too, belonged in the embrace of God's family, and that His love for me was limitless, unwavering, and unyielding.

The turning point, the epiphany that etched its mark on my spirit, occurred in 2022, within the serene walls of my family cabin nestled in the untouched beauty of northern Minnesota. There, alone with my thoughts and the whispers of the brisk November wind, I embarked on a pilgrimage of self-discovery. The words of a draft version of Briant's manuscript for this book, specifically Chapter 7—"The War Within," resonated deeply with the disquietude I sought to untangle. In the stillness of those days, I retraced my steps through the landscapes of my past, revisiting moments of isolation and of feeling like an outsider.

And then, amid my reflections, I experienced a revelation—a dawning awareness that even in those moments of profound disconnection, I had never truly been alone. The Holy Spirit revealed to me the countless instances when His presence had been by my side and when His love had shielded me from the shadows of doubt and fear. With this newfound clarity, I realized that my identity was not rooted in the imperfect relationships of this world, but in my status as a beloved child of God.

Briant's words, which had once been external affirmations, now echoed within the chambers of my heart, transforming knowledge into belief. I shared my revelation with him, and his joyous celebration only solidified the truth of what had transpired within me. In that moment of awakening, the weight of the world lifted from my shoulders, and I felt a profound sense of belonging, a profound sense of love. I was home.

The journey that Briant and I embarked on, through conversations, through introspection, and through prayer, culminated in an understanding that is as simple as it is profound: we are deeply loved, and we belong in the eternal embrace of God's grace. These truths are not mere mantras to be recited, but foundational principles that illuminate the path we walk. Briant's words, captured within the pages of this book, extend an invitation to each reader—an invitation to reclaim the original intent God had for us, to rediscover the beauty of our identity, and to embrace the fullness of life that awaits when we rest in His love.

Briant Cuffy is an intellectual, a theologian, and a philosopher. But he is much more than that. He is an authentic friend, a shepherd of hearts, a guide to those who seek solace in the arms of the divine. Through his pastoral leadership, his unwavering strength as a leader, his patient fatherhood, and his devoted love as a husband, Briant embodies the multifaceted nature of a life fully surrendered to God's grace. Above all, he is a testament to the transformative power of a soul awakened by the love of Christ.

As I reflect upon our journey—the conversations, the revelations, the shared laughter, and the shared tears—I am humbled by the privilege of knowing Briant. To call him a friend is to acknowledge the profound impact he has had on my faith, my perspective, and my very being. Through the lens of his wisdom, I have come to understand more fully that God is on our side. His love sustains us, His love empowers us, and His love illuminates the darkness.

It is my hope and my prayer that the pages that follow serve as a guide, a companion, and a source of comfort for those who journey through them. May the words within these chapters lead you back to the heart of your identity, and may they remind you of the boundless love that defines your existence. Briant's insights, born from a life deeply rooted in faith and a heart profoundly attuned to the rhythms of the divine, have the power to transform your perspective, to kindle a fire within your soul, and to set you on a path towards the fullness of life in Christ.

With gratitude for the grace that has intertwined our lives, and with anticipation for the transformative journey ahead.

—Mark Benson

Introduction

Danger was lurking in the ancient Garden. It threatened everything within reach. Adam and Eve had always thought themselves to be free, but now suddenly, their freedom was giving way to something sinister and epic in proportion. The limits of their freedom would be tested, and they could not have imagined what awaited them. But were they not listening? Adam was certainly paying attention when God brought him the woman. We know that from his heartfelt words. *"This is now bone of my bones and flesh of my flesh,"* He said. Nothing had ever made him feel this way. Then the LORD God said, *"It is not good that the man should be alone; I will make him a helper fit for him."* (Gen.2:18) Eve was made to complete Adam— she was right for him.

As his partner however, Eve would hold great influence over Adam. She had the ability to help him obey God, or help him into danger. She would soon choose the later. Eve's curiosity entangled Adam in something so dangerous that its consequences would last for all of human history. She took of the forbidden fruit and gave it also to Adam, and with a single bite, they signed away their freedom. Shame was overtaking them as they recognized for the first time where their choice had led them. They would no longer have to wonder about the limits of their freedom; *"their eyes were opened."* This exposure however, left them ridden with guilt, and isolated from God and themselves.

Since that day in Eden, (Gen.3:6) man has been trapped in a circle of unintended consequences—not unlike our first parents. Despite God's warnings, Adam and Eve found a way out of the circle of obedience. But they would soon find out that living outside God's circle was far more dangerous than they had imagined. Obedience had seemed a trap to them, but disobedience would unravel their happy home. In the creation account (Gen. 1:26) God is said to have created man in His own image and after His likeness. He had blessed them (Gen. 1:28) and gave them authority to rule, and to multiply. Yet two short chapters later the building tension between freedom and the need for danger collided, throwing the human race into a tailspin. Sin had entered the world and Adam and Eve could no longer rule.

Because they failed to rule over their hearts, the divine image was now corrupted, stained by that one single act. With a broken image, a misguided will and an eroding sense of freedom, they found themselves in a prison of their own making. Intending only to probe the possibilities, they would succeed in getting more than they bargained for. They began their day as innocent and free adventurers, but they would end up enlightened but in hiding from God and a threat to themselves. They quickly learned the two sides of danger: danger both thrills and kills.

Like Adam and Eve, we too love to play with danger. We hope and strive to add to the beauty of our lives. We enlist in the epic struggle to redefine what it means to be human. But every attempt to accelerate this adventure leaves us potentially more vulnerable. But we insist nonetheless, with haste and urgency, seeking freedom from monotony, and pleasure for our souls. But pleasure is a deceiver. It makes gamblers of us, provoking us to squander our safety for a few fading minutes in the spotlight. If life is a game, pleasure is the jack pot.

Pleasure ranks at the top in our unrelenting effort to procure a meaningful life. Every civilization seems to improve on this basic need. We hate boredom. Our creativity at inventing and improving our pleasure sources has certainly left its imprint on our souls. No one of us can escape the glaring irony of our common history. Our search for peace tends to lead to war. Our search for freedom tends to turn to vile bondage. And our search for pleasure and happiness has left us wounded where it hurts the most, in our hearts. In the end everything that man touches end up breaking because of sin.

Human enterprises betray us with the illusion that we can live without God. They make promises but fail to deliver what we seek. One enterprise alone will free us. Only God can free us. His desire is that we discover the wisdom of giving in to His demands. Otherwise, we are left groping in an ever-widening darkness; isolated and broken to the point of useless.

Seeking to mend this brokenness is the humble task of this book. The chapters that follow will be my attempt at helping you, the reader, understand that you were made for wholeness, beauty, and glory. As you read these pages, may the light of heaven bring you healing as God rewrites your story, mends your brokenness and reprints His *image* deeply upon your heart.

1

A Curious Nature

The cure for boredom is curiosity.
There is no cure for curiosity.
~ **Dorothy Parker** *(1893–1967) (attributed)*

uriosity is dangerous. The most natural human instinct is the desire to transcend the common life. Curiosity is our tour guide, but when it takes over, boundaries are both blurred and ignored, often beyond recognition. The excitement of new things tends to leave us wanting more, and the desire for *more* can be the greatest enemy of our safety.

It seems to be part of human nature to never be satisfied with anything whatsoever. You give a man happiness, and he will become drunk with it. Give him freedom, and he will abuse it. Give him knowledge, and he will use it to explain his sin. The paradox to our condition is that the expected cure of our curiosity causes us to be more desperate and dangerous. Unlike God, who is infinite and free, we are bound even by progress. Yet we have something so very important in common with God.

Some years ago, an avalanche was triggered within me when someone stated, "God is dangerous." My senses fluttered. In the days that followed, I spent hours thinking about what it meant. I soon discovered that God's dangerous nature is imprinted upon our hearts. This is where danger is redefined from a negative to a positive. Being created in His *likeness* means that we share God's appetite for danger: a righteous fury and bold confidence that stirs our sense of adventure, awakens our passions, and fills us with creativity. When He carved us from the dust, God created something *good* and—may I dare say—*dangerous*. But we would be foolish to confuse this dangerous appetite for independence. As the eaglet must learn to fly in the shadow of the experienced eagle, so we must be dangerous within the shadow of the Almighty. In that instance, danger is not a threat to our freedom but the passage into a life that sets us free.

God makes us uncomfortable. He turns our world upside down and redefines our lives. He is a fire that threatens and burns away our selfishness and greed and replaces them with holy contentment. He launches us into the deep, uncertain mystery of divine providence. But who among us really wants this? Still, the eternal Father, the Creator of all things, bothers with us, that He might have our hearts and make us skillful in doing the dangerous work ordained for us from the beginning. God's great undertaking is to carve our hearts into the shape of freedom. The world also offers freedom, but at the high cost of disobedience. *Be a law unto yourself! Be your own freedom! Be your own god!* the world cries. However, the risk, the dangerous risk, is to trust God enough to walk in obedience on the unseen and very real path of freedom. This freedom promises to be infinitely better than anything the world has yet seen or experienced. It is achieved through obedience, which explains why Satan's visit to Eden was so full of consequence for Adam and for humanity.

A STRANGER IN THE GARDEN

Nobody likes to feel trapped, and that included Adam and Eve. But they had a choice. They did not have to disobey. At first, Eden was the only place they ever wanted to be because they had nothing to compare it to. All that would change when they began to experience discontentment. But how could they? God Himself planted a garden for them: *"And the LORD God planted a garden in Eden, in the east, and there he put the man whom he had formed. And out of the ground the LORD God made to spring up every tree that is pleasant to the sight and good for food. The tree of life was in the midst of the garden, and the tree of the knowledge of good and evil"* (Genesis 2:8–9 ESV). Gordon Talbot in his commentary on Genesis noted: "The tree of knowledge of good and evil reminded Adam of his need to be obedient to God."[1] Every time they saw the tree, they were to remember their spiritual duty to obey their Creator. God also gave Adam a job.

Eve had a home, a husband, and a lovely garden. She had all the things she could have wanted. Best of all, Adam and Eve had God, who walked with them during the best part of the day. But something within them could not escape the feeling that they were trapped inside a circle of innocence. They had a free will and the ability to act within or against their own interests. No one made them eat of the fruit of the Tree of Knowledge of Good and Evil; they chose to eat. It was the most consequential choice in all of history. Most discussions about original sin completely disregard the fact that sin is *always* up to us. We are free moral agents, but our choices have consequences. Free agents can act in ways that defy reason, especially when they face the drag of familiarity. Our love for adventure, romance, and comedy are windows into this yearning to escape boredom.

Adam and Eve began this curious quest, and the conflict continues today. Being in a perfect situation with all they could have ever wanted was not enough. Eden was overlaid with rushing rivers, majestic mountains, beautiful plants, and fascinating animals. Furthermore, they had each other, with timeless simplicity and innocence. What else could one ask for? Still, the storyline of Genesis describes two people trapped in a conundrum between perfect beauty, a holy God, and free will. Let's not forget for a moment God's single command: *"The LORD God commanded the man, saying, 'From any tree of the garden you may eat freely; but from the tree of the knowledge of good and evil you shall not eat, for in the day that you eat from it you will surely die'"* (Genesis 2:16–17 NASB).

Adam and his wife, Eve, failed to uphold God's explicit command and found out through disobedience what was intended to be gained through obedience. In their commentary on Genesis, Keil and Delitzsch argued, "According to the divine intention, this was to be attained through his not eating of its fruit."[2] There was nothing evil about the Tree of Knowledge. The problem was that they disobeyed. They wanted freedom but chose to find it the wrong way. True freedom would be found in obeying God. Up until that time, Adam and Eve had been fully content with God, fully free. Then a stranger paid them a visit. They were familiar only with the voice of God who created them and demanded their obedient love. Now, for the first time, they were listening to the voice of God's enemy, and he led them astray through their natural curiosity.

They never imagined what havoc their audience with the Serpent of Paradise would wreak upon human history. Still one wonders, why did they act against their own best interest and jeopardize their safe and glorious fellowship with their Creator? Their behavior provides an important clue into the danger that threatens all who share the nature of Adam: they were risk takers. They did not like *safe*, and they didn't fully appreciate *glorious*. It is as if God's pleasures had grown cold in light of their wondering minds.

Satan's most formidable weapon is his ability to deceive us with the illusion that there is something to be gained beyond God. The moment we believe this, we become emboldened to the point of risking everything, no matter how high the cost. The voice of God may be loud or soft, a whisper or a shout, but it is never conniving. Satan, however, wrote the script on deceit. He is known for his ability to trick humans into doubting God. John 8:44 says, *"Whenever he speaks a lie, he speaks from his own nature, for he is a liar and the father of lies"* (NASB). He is dedicated to deceiving men into believing anything but the whole truth— and Adam and Eve were about to take his bait.

Returning to our story in Genesis 3, we find the Serpent, or Satan, getting ready to make his move. The Bible says in verse 1: *"Now the serpent was craftier than any beast of the field which the LORD God had made. And he said to the woman, 'Indeed, has God said, "You shall not eat from any tree of the garden"?'"* (Genesis 3:1 NASB). Satan knew something about Eve that she did not know about herself. He knew that if offered a chance to explore the possibilities, she would find the temptation irresistible. It is noteworthy that Satan makes the pitch to Eve, not Adam. I have often wondered about that. It seems that Satan knew something about the basic nature of the woman. He knew that Eve was the more emotional one and therefore more susceptible for the kind of deception he had in mind. Let me stop at this point and make an important clarification. I do not mean to suggest that women are more easily given to temptation. Instead, I mean to say that Eve's basic instinct was to experience the feeling rather than to ponder the consequences of her action.

Women, don't be offended that you are more emotionally wired than men. God created you that way by design. Satan was only using his knowledge of God's work, and Eve was willing to play. But sin did not begin with Eve eating the fruit that God told her and her husband not to eat. Sin began in her heart, the seat of her emotion. Satan made her question the basic goodness of God. She became suspicious of God's motive and generosity. Then the Serpent invited her to explore with her emotions what she was curious about. All temptation is like that. It appeals to the need within us for pleasure, happiness, or some kind of fulfillment we feel we are lacking. The sinful act offers us a way of achieving the pleasure, happiness, or fulfillment we seek. Eve began to imagine the benefits and forgot to ponder the cost.

Everything in life comes at a cost. Business executives know all too well the need to analyze cost and benefit. Before they set out to sell a product, they (1) do a cost analysis, (2) design the product to appeal to potential buyers, and (3) calculate the payoff. Satan had done his homework, and resistance for Eve was an uphill battle. It appears that she looked at the benefits and forgot to analyze the cost. That was her problem. But where was Adam in all this? Did he leave the important and unscheduled meeting with Satan to the woman? Or was Adam present but never said a word? We can't be certain about the answers to these questions. Scripture makes no mention of Adam being present, but we'll assume he was not involved in the conversation. One thing is certain: God was displaced from their affection (at least for that moment), and Satan moved in for the kill.

RESTLESS LONGINGS

Fantasies are great in movies and daydreams but more than disappointing in real life. Nothing can ever truly fill us until our hearts are conditioned by simplicity—the act of enjoying what we have rather than what we wish for. Fantasies may delight us, but only for a short time, and they must soon be replaced by newer, more exciting possibilities. Old toys don't hold their appeal. Think about this for yourself. At first, we love to play with our new toys, both as children and as grown adults. The new house and the new car last for only so long before the shine wears off. Then it's time to find something else with a *new* smell. Those who maintain excitement and continue to enjoy life with *older* things are wise—they know that everything grows old eventually, and old can be better. For such people, simplicity is sacred.

If you want to measure a man's greatness, don't look at how much he needs to keep him happy; look at how little makes him happy. The more a man is satisfied with sacred simplicity, the less he wants. And the less a man wants, the more he has to give—even his little is plenty. But he who longs for more as a means of contentment lives with his hands stretched out and his heart stretched in. Nothing ever really satisfies such a person. He goes from one quest to another, never finding what only God can provide. Although we were made for enjoyment, nothing must ever rival our love for our Creator.

Saint Augustine has said it plainly: "He has made us with eternity in our hearts. And our hearts are restless until they find their rest in Him."[3] Restless! That's a good way to describe us, is it not? I am convinced with Scripture that only God really understands our hearts: *"Thus says the LORD, 'Let not a wise man boast of his wisdom, and let not the mighty man boast of his might, let not a rich man boast of his riches; but let him who boasts boast of this, that he understands and knows Me, that I am the Lord who exercises lovingkindness, justice and righteousness on earth; for I delight in these things,' declares the LORD"* (Jeremiah 9:23–24 NASB). Each of us knows the sordid thoughts and feelings nestled within the private walls of our lives—where our private and public personas are strangers. God is in the business of remaking us into our true selves. What else will fill this empty space we call our hearts and drive away the darkness that blinds us?

Millennia after Adam, God offered this injunction to the Hebrew nation: *"You shall not make for yourself an idol, or any likeness of what is in heaven above or on the earth beneath or in the water under the earth. You shall not worship them or serve them; for I, the LORD your God, am a jealous God, visiting the iniquity of the fathers on the children and on the third and fourth generations of those who hate me"* (Deuteronomy 5:8–9 NASB). God's warning to Israel was not a simple prohibition but a call to live in obedience. He wanted them to know without doubt or contradiction that their hearts belonged to Him alone. God is jealous for our hearts.

Like the nation of Israel, we tend to comfort ourselves with tangible things—things we can touch, smell, and handle. God does not fit that description, and for that reason, we find Him at times difficult to obey. In His absence we create idols, substitutes that serve only to further enslave our hearts and corrupt our imagination. This leaves us spiritually crippled and morally chained. God's call to obedience is the only means to perfection. But who wants to be perfect? Not Adam and Eve; not you and me. We love living on the edge. Something about the human condition makes us believe that we are more alive when things are messy and unpredictable. We humans don't like monotony.

Consider all the things that Adam and Eve gave up for a chance at adventure. First, they were willing to give up God's presence, their occupation, and ultimately their freedom. Before the Fall, Adam and Eve were complete in ways we can't imagine. They were living in the most perfect situation. Giving all this up for a chance to know what else was out there had to be the second greatest scandal in history, rivaled only by the great sacrifice of the Second Adam, Jesus Christ, who gave up His glory with the Father to die and face rejection by sinners. But did Adam and Eve know what they were giving up? They were not giving up something good for something better. They gave up something great for something evil. That's the choice we make in giving up a close relationship with God for an uncertain slice of pleasure. They went from walking with God in blissful innocence and ruling over His work to hiding from His presence. But God made them to rule. Beneath the chaos of history is the most ignored fact of our humanity: we were made to rule with God. But sinning against God displaced them, and slavery would now ensue.

It was perhaps a spring day in the Garden of Eden when God came looking. His voice thundered with urgency; "Adam, where are you?" Brushing past every other created thing, God made His way to that place in Eden where He and Adam had met many times for conversation and mutual delight. But Adam and Eve were not there: *"And they heard the sound of the LORD God walking in the garden in the cool of the day, and the man and his wife hid themselves from presence of the LORD God among the trees of the garden. But the LORD God called to the man and said to him, 'Where are you?'"* (Genesis 3:8–9 ESV). Can you imagine what that was like? Something terribly cynical is going on here.

First, let us agree that God knew where Adam and Eve were; He was not gathering information. Instead, God was pointing out the obvious: they were hiding. Something was wrong, and both they and God knew it, but only God was willing to confront it. "Where are you?" is God's invitation to Adam to acknowledge wrong and to seek restoration. But the next verse takes our breath away. Adam said, *"I heard the sound of you in the garden, and I was afraid, because I was naked, and I hid myself"* (Genesis 3:10 ESV). But wait. Adam's answer begs the question. Adam's reason for hiding was his nakedness. But he was always naked; that's how they did things in Eden. Why is Adam suddenly self-conscious? He was now exposed after eating the forbidden fruit. His eyes were opened as God spoke and shame entered Adam's heart. That was the first indication of their loss of innocence. But there would be more to come.

Never had they felt the need to hide from God. Guilt and shame were quickly overtaking them. Adam offered yet another reason for his hiding; he was *afraid.* Why did he feel so afraid? Was it a fear of God's penalty? Was it fear of the Serpent? Were they mostly afraid to do anything else to further jeopardize their lives? God's inquisition continued in verse 11 when He asked: *"Who told you that you were naked? Have you eaten of the tree of which I commanded you not to eat?"* Great question: "Who told you that you were naked?"

Adam may have been trying to find an answer to God's question, but before he said a word, God had a follow up: *"Have you eaten of the tree of which I commanded you not to eat?"* Ah, now he had to answer directly. No room for crafty answers or long explanations. Adam must now speak. What will he say this time? Not so surprisingly, he answers: *"The woman whom you gave to be with me, she gave me fruit of the tree, and I ate"* (v. 12). Things are not going well for Adam. God expected that he would take responsibility and admit his wrong with brokenness and humility, but that was not the story of our father Adam. All he had to say was, "I am sorry." God knew what really happened, so telling a lie seems as strange as his first answer about why he was hiding.

Adam was not the only one who tried to save his own skin that day. God turned to the woman next: *"Then the LORD said to the woman, 'What is this that you have done?'"* (Genesis 3:13).

Eve replied, *"The serpent deceived me, and I ate."* They were playing the blame game in the Garden of Eden before their God. Sovereign and mighty as He is, God already had a plan. It had been a long, dramatic day in Eden with heavy consequence for humanity.

In one day, sin entered the world, Adam and Eve went into hiding, and then they blamed their sin on each other and the Serpent. No one took direct responsibility. But what made it possible for Satan to break through Adam's defenses? If we can answer that question, we will discover what imprisons us. Like Adam, we are fighting the same battle, wrestling with the same tempter, and the solution to our problem is the same. We are asking a question for which there is no answer anywhere but in God. So why did Adam miss it? What kept him from knowing that he was in danger? The answer will surprise you.

OUT OF POST

After receiving instructions from God in Genesis chapter 1, Adam made one simple but fatal mistake: he forgot to guard his heart. But why, you may ask, did he need to guard his heart? Eden was a perfect place, so why should he have any suspicion that Satan was up to evil? While it's true that Adam on the surface would not have known the Serpent's strategy, he failed to heed the voice of God. He failed to stand and fight for his heart. Adam failed to fight for the heart of his wife, Eve.

To say this simply, Adam made a gamble and learned that no one ever gambles on life without paying the price. All of humanity follows Adam down that road. We play with fate and dance with danger. We gamble our futures with no thought of tomorrow. And then tomorrow comes. The first place we fail to rule is our hearts. Before a man can rule his home, finances, or other people, he must first rule his heart—otherwise, he has nothing to offer this world. This is the sounding alarm to all who will listen. It rings from the echoes of Eden to the whispers and shouts of mature men. Its message is clear and urgent: *"Watch over your heart with all diligence, for from it flow the springs of life"* (Proverbs 4:23 NASB).

Jacob Needleman, author of *Why Can't We Be Good?* punctuates this plea: "The main outstanding discovery, is that I am—we are—obliged by the power of conscience, the source of all moral authority, to care for our I-*ness*, which is our attention. It may, in fact, be possible, to say that for us modern people all genuine ethical responsibility begins there, with this entirely new, or hidden, responsibility to my Self. I cannot be responsible to you without being responsible to my Self—to let it live in me."[4] Needleman is right. If we wish to bring about good, to rule over the evil we see, we must first rule over our hearts. Responsibility is pivotal to this effort.

With our hearts we win and lose. With our hearts we deliberate and decide. Character is the outcome of these actions. A man of character can persuade without violence, force, or anger. Such a man loves his duties, asks for nothing, and gives to others. His wants are few and his joys are many. This is the man you want as neighbor, friend, and brother—the man you would fear as a foe.

Apart from Jesus, no other man in history could be as great as Adam. For starters, he was made sinless. He had no sin and therefore no limits to his creative, physical, and intellectual powers. Satan hated Adam and wanted to destroy him. Never forget that Satan's hate is always first against God. He puts God on notice wherever great men are. In the first chapter of Job, we see the same rivalry building in the fight for Job's heart. As we enter the dialogue in heaven, God introduces his servant Job: *"There was a man in the land of Uz whose name was Job, and that man was blameless and upright, one who feared God and turned away from evil"* (Job 1:1 esv). Before God was through introducing him, Satan wanted a crack at Job. This man who was perfect and upright was much too dangerous; he had to be lowered and diminished. He had to be troubled by any means possible until he tripped. But Job nurtured his faith with God and esteemed it above everything else. He was responsible.

Grave dangers have befallen God's people when they fail to stay at their post and own their hearts. When we forsake our calling, bad things happen. Leaders of religious and secular influence have far too often fallen by this vice. Forsaking to guard their responsibility, they wander into a wilderness where they lack the strength to resist sin's many invites. One of the lessons from this expedition is the folly of thinking that by ignoring God's command, one has something to gain. It is foolish to forsake the only thing worth keeping for things that are passing. The true warrior is the one who knows his role on the battlefield and follows his champion in the line of fire. For such a man, losing his life is not his greatest loss. For this man, losing everything is defined by dying while following his own designs rather than those of his warrior king. It's strange how we love to wander; stranger yet is how long it takes us to get the lesson that to *wander* is to be out of post.

But why do we love to wander? I believe it is because something in us wants to see what else is out there. While thinking about this very thing one day, it came to me in a calm whisper that satisfaction depends on obedience. The key to obedience is to love God more than self.

I can personally testify to times in my own life when the need to strike out took me down a path of much regret. I recall one such instance in the summer of 1987. About twenty of us students decided to make a trip to the Boiling Lake in my home country of Dominica. After what seemed to be forever (three hours on the trail), we finally reached the last tip of the journey that would lead us down the Valley of Desolation (a dreadful swamp of burning lava), just half an hour from the Boiling Lake. It was at that time that some of us decided to take a shortcut to our destination. But things didn't turn out as planned. By the time we got there, everyone in the group was leaving to make it back before dark. We never had the chance to enjoy the trip. We had endured long winding trails, lots of mosquito bites, blisters, cuts along the way, passages through tight crevices between rocks, and a looming precipice. (Our entire adventure was derailed.)

I learned something that day. I learned that detours give no guarantee of enjoyment or safe arrival. Adam and Eve learned that lesson too. Their decision to ignore God's map changed the dynamic of their relationship and eventually led to their slow but certain death. That's how far we humans go to disobey, and in so doing, we dispose of blessings that could be ours through obedience.

God is still calling the sons and daughters of Adam to come out of hiding and face their Maker. He still asks with urgent thunder, "Where are you?" The challenge is not in hearing what God is saying but in doing it. It doesn't matter whether the disobedience is outright or delayed. They both qualify as disobedience.

VAIN IMAGINATIONS

Whatever controls our imagination will also control our lives. We are bound to act out of our motives, impressions, and ideas. Whatever we imagine will find its way out of our thoughts, feelings, and actions. And we must always remember that imagination has a life and mind of its own. With time and opportunity, no fate is too steep for humanity to conceive, as Adam and Eve revealed. They allowed their minds to wander and to stray into forbidden places. An imagination once ruled by innocence was now controlled by indulgence and skepticism about God. What prevailed then, and in every succeeding generation, was an all-too-familiar egoism along with the repercussion it brings. Satan knew that and his strategy was brilliant. He knew Adam and Eve had found great pleasure with God, for it says that they walked with Him in the cool of the day. That means they enjoyed the best part of every day with God. Nothing made them more alive than being with their Creator.

But Satan got them to believe a lie by asking, "Is God really enough?" In a garden so wide, with so many wonderful things to see and eat, they began to doubt what God told them. Would they play it safe? As Adam and Eve pondered the question, they began imagining what awaited them beyond the familiar world in which God was King. He was the king of their desires, expectations, and pleasures. But imagination was quickly taking over, and before long, it would morph into compromise.

Adam and Eve show us why imagination must be guarded by conviction, tempered with humility, and motivated by love. They had come to the edge of something dangerous. *What else could God be keeping from us?* they wondered. But their problem remained even after they had fulfilled their desire. That had to be the greatest letdown—giving up abundant goodness for something that left them wanting and more alone than ever before. That's the problem with desire: it has a beginning, but it has no end. The moment we open ourselves to things unapproved by God, sin's chains bind our hearts and a saga of sorrow ensues.

Three lessons emerge from the story of Adam and Eve. First, the heart is dangerously curious and capable of great deception. Second, temptation will find us wherever we are. And third, what we desire the most may also be what we should steadfastly avoid. It is precarious to love anything that is not God. Adam and his wife began to love their own lives and pleasures above God. Their actions haunt our common history. God cannot be shared or mingled with anything. The moment we begin to imagine something other than Him, we become vulnerable to lies and open to deceit. And our enemy, whose mission is our demise, waits in hidden silence.

2

False Promises

Enemies' promises were made to be broken.
~ Aesop

S atan is a liar who has mastered his craft. It is just
as impossible for him to tell the truth as it is for
God to tell a lie. And lies are dangerous, not only
because they mislead us, but also because they destroy
our confidence in the truth about God and ourselves.
We become cynics who doubt the truth and believe a
lie. One of the greatest lies ever told was Satan's lie to
Adam and Eve: *"You will be like God, knowing good
and evil"* (Genesis 3:5 ESV). It was true that they would
know good and evil, but that would not make them
like God. Satan knew all too well how outrageously
false his "promise" was, but it should not surprise us;
he is the father of lies. His imagination is ruled by
falsehoods. He is the enemy of truth, and he opposes
God. He accused Adam and Eve whom God loved.
No tactic was too diabolical, twisted, or false that he
would not employ. His method was *The end will justify
the means*, but both the end and the means violated
their safety.

What Adam and Eve needed was to know God and to be known by Him. But Satan skewed their thinking and converted their desire to know God into a selfish ambition to be like God instead. Being like God? Did Satan really believe his own promise? He had tried to overrule God and was forced out of heaven. But Satan is a determined foe who stops at nothing. What better way to undermine God but to mar the apple of His eyes by turning their hearts from Him? Their attentiveness was exactly what he needed. He had entered the sacred chamber of their hearts, and his false promise led them to believe something that was both unattainable and dangerous.

There's a German proverb that says, "One must have a good memory to be able to keep the promises one makes." In Satan's case, he not only had a bad memory, but he also had bad blood. He had stood in praise of God (*"How you have fallen from heaven, morning star, son of the dawn! You have been cast down to the earth, you who once laid low the nations!"* [Isaiah 14:12 NIV]) but was himself tired of singing the praises of God; he wanted what was God's alone. His ambition was to take the throne of God by whatever means possible. Why? He was given great influence and access to God. Would all that be enough? Listen:

> *The word of the LORD came to me: "Son of man, take up a lament concerning the king of Tyre and say to him: 'This is what the Sovereign LORD says: "You were the seal of perfection, full of wisdom and*

perfect in beauty. You were in Eden, the garden of
God; every precious stone adorned you: carnelian,
chrysolite and emerald, topaz, onyx and jasper,
lapis lazuli, turquoise and beryl. Your settings and
mountings were made of gold; on the day you were
created they were prepared. You were anointed as
a guardian cherub, for so I ordained you. You were
on the holy mount of God; you walked among the
fiery stones."" (Ezekiel 28:11–14 NIV)

As you listen, you will hear a lot of past-tense language. Five times in these verses, God reminded Satan of all he ignored for a "chance" to be like God. You *were* a model of perfection. You *were* in the garden of God, a place of beauty on all sides, a place of enjoyment. You *were* anointed by God as a guardian cherub. You *were* on the holy mount of God and walked among the fiery stones. Satan was an archangel, like Michael or Gabriel, whose ego became too inflated. Heaven was not a big enough stage for Satan to share with his Creator.

After God forced Satan out from His presence, his mission became the destruction of God's precious earth and its inhabitants, Adam and Eve. He entered the garden with a diabolical mission of deception, and Eve was the prime target. He thought, "If I told them the truth, they would believe me, and in so doing would obey God. I will tell them a lie." The truth would lead them to God; a lie would lead them away. He would do nothing that would help God's cause. The consequences for Satan's rebellion would not be shared alone; he was looking to enlist others to both rebel and share his misery. As the old saying goes, "Misery likes company." Satan wanted company.

LIES THAT BIND

Satan knew exactly what he was doing—tell a lie so ripe with consequences that all of heaven and earth would feel its impact. He got it done. Yes, Satan accomplished his mission. Adam and Eve listened to a lie that would bind their hearts and those of all generations to follow. Sin's seed was firmly planted. Lying would become a habit of the heart: creating distrust, causing friction on a horizontal scale, and digging an ever-widening vertical chasm between God and His created beings. Let us revisit the crime scene in Eden and continue observing Satan's artful deception. *"Now the serpent was more crafty than any other beast of the field that the LORD God had made. He said to the woman, 'Did God actually say, "You shall not eat of any tree in the garden"?'"* (Genesis 3:1 ESV). He knew full well what God had said. But his aim was to plant doubt about God's motive because he knew that second guessing God would lead to rash behavior.

Eve engaged Satan in the next two verses: *"And the woman said to the serpent, 'We may eat of the fruit of the trees in the garden, but God said, "You shall not eat of the fruit of the tree that is in the midst of the garden, neither shall you touch it, lest you die"'"* (Genesis 3:2–3 ESV). Eve gave a good answer. She was quoting God, but would that be enough? God was very clear that they should neither touch nor eat of a particular tree—the tree that was in the midst of the garden. *"But the serpent said to the woman, 'You will not surely die'"* (Genesis 3:4). In his typical form, Satan's lie was vicious, deliberate, and contrary to God's own words.

Words have meaning and actions have consequences. God's words were not only direct, but they also carried with them the consequence of death. Lying words build false promises that lead to false choices. The false choice offered to Eve was that she could disobey God without consequence—God was not serious. But it turned out that God was serious about sin, and sinners would have to pay. God warns us to listen and obey His commands, not because He hates fun, but because He hates sin. There is a difference. Pastor and author John Piper notes, "Sin is what you do when your heart is not satisfied with God."[5] Sin promises to satisfy, but it leaves a larger hole in the heart that seeks pleasure outside of God. It is fun to love God with a whole heart because there is nothing greater to seek after. Fun was what Adam and Eve already had and did not know it. Sin was what they thought would be fun, but it ended up destroying their fun. Sin is a trap. A trap is set to capture prey. Satan is intent on capturing hearts. His promises are baits for our capture. Obey them and miss the thrill of God's holy pleasure.

Before Adam and Eve knew it, Satan had stolen their attention, and one last thing was in order. He promised that they would be like God, and they believed him: *"For God knows that when you eat of it your eyes will be opened, and you will be like God, knowing good and evil"* (Genesis 3:5). Adam and Eve could never become like God, not even through perfect obedience, far less through disobedience. The person of God is too immense for human imitation and ascendancy. To be like God is quite a hefty flight up the human ladder. On our very best day, we are like bugs in a field of elephants. When pride enters the sacred spaces of the heart, false promises give root to flawed, unsteady actions, which lead to certain demise. Adam and Eve's eyes were indeed opened but not to good—evil descended upon them like a vicious darkness. It also did not help that they were not *like God*, as Satan had promised. In this exists the danger of following after lies—they may seem plausible with their false glitter, but they never live up to expectations.

In the first lie, Satan had only aroused their interest. With the next move, he set their passions aflame, and from that point on, there was no turning back. They were now wandering in territory that was both restricted and dangerous. The mystery they so desperately longed for had now come to their door, yet they were afraid. Why? Because mystery is mysterious for a reason; it is not meant to be known. Adam and Eve came too close and lost their sense of mystery. And when you lose your sense of mystery, God is mistaken as human, and human is mistaken as divine.

UNREACHABLE HEIGHTS

On a flight from Dallas, Texas, to Richmond, Virginia, I experienced the awesome realization of wonder. At 30,000 feet in the air, our flight began to experience some turbulence. I am, for the most part, very calm during travel. On that occasion, however, I was a bit concerned, partly because my girlfriend (now my wife) sitting next to me began holding onto my hands for dear life. Obviously, I continued to pretend that I had no fear while I panicked on the inside. It did not help when the lady two seats in front of us loudly asked the couple to her left, "Is our wing on fire?" I turned to observe my girlfriend's face; she was in a state of panic. I tried to smile but ended up only forcing a modest grin.

The situation became outright stressful for most of the passengers. Lightning flashed and lit up the sky as far as our eyes could see. I was so impressed with the lightning storm that I leaned into the window, pressing in for a good view, while Carrie kept her eyes shut at my request. I kept thinking, "What majesty is here in this threatening storm. What power!" I noticed many others watching the storm. After what seemed an eternity, and to everyone's delight, we finally landed. The lady who thought the wing was on fire walked out of the plane and went her own way, along with all the other passengers. We followed. But why was my attention glued to this event in the sky? It reminded me of God, the greatest wonder in the universe. He is like that lightning storm—His wonder is magnificent and beautiful to watch, but it is dangerous to approach.

Scripture tells us, *"Our God is a consuming fire"* (Hebrews 12:29 ESV). He burns with such violence and power that no one wants to take Him for granted. Yet, like Adam and Eve, we all take God for granted. We look at His majesty and feel nothing—no fear, no awe, no amazement. We have become hardened by a false sense of who God is. We have such a high view of ourselves that we refuse to see that God is not only our hope, but also our very life, breath, and destiny. It would do us good to remember the infinite distance between us and the Divine.

SACRED SPACES

"Know your place." We've heard those words many times over the course of our lives. It means to stay within your allotted space and be satisfied with what you have, not what you wish you had. It means that God created us all to live within the boundaries and spaces where we can be fruitful and produce the lives meant for us. That's a hard idea to digest because we don't like staying within our sacred spaces. We are wanderers. We like to wander off and play with the wishes and longings of our sinful, restless hearts.

I have learned this lesson far too many times in the course of my life. One shining example takes me back to my childhood. My mom told me not to leave her side as she talked with a neighbor one afternoon. As the conversation was prolonged, I got bored, became tired of waiting, and wandered away. She warned me because she was protecting me, but I wanted no protection. I wanted to stray. I will never forget the price I had to pay for wandering that day. Before long, I came back screaming from bee stings to my face and arms. I was hurting. I wandered too far from her safe reach. That day, I learned that when you stray from your sacred space, bad things can happen. Danger may seem appealing, but in the end, it's never worth the consequences of our disobedience. Adam and Eve felt the sting of that lesson.

Where did that attitude come from? It is etched into our nature. We cannot help ourselves; we are human, and we rebel. But angels do too. Listen to God's account of Satan's rebellion, which led to our downfall:

You were blameless in your ways from the day you were created till wickedness was found in you. Through your widespread trade you were filled with violence, and you sinned. So I drove you in disgrace from the mount of God, and I expelled you, guardian cherub, from among the fiery stones. Your heart became proud on account of your beauty, and you corrupted your wisdom because of your splendor. So I threw you to the earth; I made a spectacle of you before kings. By your many sins and dishonest trade you have dese-crated your sanctuaries. So I made a fire come out from you, and it consumed you, and I reduced you to ashes on the ground in the sight of all who were watching. All the nations who knew you are appalled at you; you have come to a horrible end and will be no more. (Ezekiel 28:15–19 NIV)

The righteous indignation of God is unmistakable. God discloses how Satan lost his honor by wickedness, pride, violence, corrupt wisdom, and dishonesty. In other words, Satan allowed it to "go to his head." The Serpent used his knowledge of the truth to deceive with malicious intent. He corrupted the truth for his purposes. Inflamed by his pride, he mounted an assault on his Creator. That enraged God so much that He made a shameful spectacle of his rebellion, deposing him before the hosts of heaven and casting him down in hot displeasure. Satan conceived a plan to draw Adam and Eve into the same isolation that was dealt him by his Creator.

Unlike angels, however, humans have a chance at redemption. Jesus did not die for angels; He died for humans. God would restore Adam and Eve, although He did not save them from the just penalty of their sin. He covered them and protected them from further doom, and in the course of time, He sent a Redeemer to save their sons and daughters from His holy wrath.

Their rebellion was costly, not only to us, but also to God. It cost Him His only begotten Son. If we understand the utter awfulness of sin, it helps us see why Satan worked so hard to deceive our first parents. If he could get them outside their sacred space, he could make them an easy target, and that they were. They were dissatisfied with all that God was, but wandering away from Him would take them into an unholy space and lasting dissatisfaction.

Satan managed to make Adam and Eve believe in the very thing for which he was dethroned: they would be *like God*. Adam and Eve were to obey God, keep the garden, and produce offspring who would continue to reproduce righteousness in and beyond Eden. All that changed with Satan's lie. They now wanted to attempt what Satan failed to achieve: they wanted to be like God. Brazen, is it not? Yet none of us should be surprised that when we step outside our sacred space, we oppose God and threaten our safety. Satan had driven a wedge between God and His human creatures that still stalks us today. We hate to admit it, but we are stalked by the ever-present danger of sin that both deceives and enslaves us, even when we are ignorant of it. Eden has left its mark on our hearts. We know we can never be like God, but we like to try.

TO KNOW AND BE KNOWN

God must be unrivaled in our allegiances, affections, and delights. Adam and Eve first failed when they imagined something better than the One True God. This is a pivotal point for reflection. Imagination is a good thing, but only if it imagines what is good and true and lovely. Setting our minds on anything that does not have its basis in God is to imagine a vain thing. That was their mistake. The first commandment makes this plain: *"You shall have no other gods before me"* (Exodus 20:3 NIV). The challenge of history is submitting to this ancient command. Since Adam and Eve, we have all failed this test. Thinking of Him and desiring Him as our true delight must always be our task.

God holds in His face (2 Corinthians 4:6) the light we seek to guide us, the grace we need to keep us, and the love we need to hold us. Imagination spent on anything outside of God is a waste. But with God as our subject, we play in the fields of eternity, are captured by the light of heaven, and are taken to a life that shines beyond our human darkness. And who could exchange that for vain things? We would. In fact, we do, repeatedly. Whether it is the allure of a delicious fruit (opening our eyes to the knowledge of good and evil), a golden calf, or the idols we invent every day, there is no end to our insatiable and desperate longings. We do this largely through our imagination, which lacks neither limit nor ambition, in the lonely quest for grandeur.

But our minds were created to imagine nothing greater than God. What we are seeking is to know God and to be known by Him. The testimony of Scripture (Jeremiah 9:23–24; Galatians 4:12; Psalm 18:28) bears this out. Jeremiah 9:23–24 cautions, *"Thus says the LORD: 'Let not the wise man boast in his wisdom, let not the mighty man boast in his might, let not the rich man boast in his riches, but let him who boasts boast in this, that he understands and knows me, that I am the LORD who practices steadfast love, justice, and righteousness in*

the earth. For in these things I delight, declares the LORD*"'*
(ESV). We were made to know and understand the
Almighty. God goes on to say that He practices what
He preaches. God fulfills His every promise. His character, His words, and His works all sing to the same
tune of justice and righteousness for all. He is for us,
not against us. Did you hear that? God is for us. He
wants us to know Him.

Even greater than knowing God is to be known by
Him. It is true that the highest function of the human
mind is to consider its best subject: God. To be known
by God is an entirely different idea. It does not mean
that God is still getting to know us—He knows all
things. It means we've been qualified by God Himself
to partake in the life-giving experience of knowing
Him. It also conveys the idea that to be known by
Him is of infinite value. It's one thing to say we know
someone and entirely another when that person also
knows us.

I once attended a party where no one except the
host knew me. As I approached the gate of the apart-
ment complex, I was stopped by a guy whose job was
to deny entry to uninvited people. As he was asking
me to confirm my identity, my friend came along. She
waved and smiled, and I was allowed to enter. I made
it past the gate and into the fellowship and friendship
of someone who knew me. To be known by God is like
that. He can testify and attest to who we are. We are
His. How beautiful is that? God knows me. He knows
you. We have passed before the eyes of Him whose

justice matters. *"Who is to condemn? Christ Jesus is the one who died—more than that, who was raised—who is at the right hand of God, who indeed is interceding for us"* (Romans 8:34 ESV). No one else can validate or invalidate us. Our identity is anchored in God. If Adam and Eve had known that, maybe their story could have ended differently.

Another hallmark of being known by God is that we love Him. *"But if anyone loves God, he is known by God"* (1 Corinthians 8:3 ESV). Here it is again—those who love God are themselves known by Him. This is reciprocal love. Those who show they love God with their heart, mind, soul, and strength will reap the benefits of safety, peace, and satisfaction. Adam and Eve certainly knew God. But were they continually growing in that knowledge? This leads us into the heart of their dilemma. God is infinite. Knowing Him is a timeless, patient, continual, and ever-unfolding enterprise. It is filled with excitement, romance, and wonder. But cynics don't have patience, and impatience skews reason. God represents an eternal and infinite knowledge that leads to life. Satan was offering Adam and Eve a chance to have their filling now. Most of us think the same way. Forever is too long to wait, even if the one who promises is faithful. We would rather take it *now* from a liar and a thief whose entire mission is to deceive and destroy.

The holy rafts of God are sent out daily to the drowning sons of Adam. God's pursuit of His people is unrelenting. But will we be rescued, or will we drift through curiosity and false promises? It is said that curiosity kills the cat, but it also kills the dream, and what is life without a dream?

God is calling us daily. He shouts and whispers and pleads. He sees us drifting and sends His ships to rescue us. But the world keeps calling, and we answer. We heed its invitation and follow its prince, but we expect the safety, peace, and satisfaction promised us by God. His intentions for us are good: *"For I know the plans I have for you, declares the LORD, plans for welfare and not for evil, to give you a future and a hope"* (Jeremiah 29:11 ESV). Why, then, do we trade in our holy robes for the dirty rags of unrighteousness? Why do we listen to the voice of a hostile stranger with a sordid past over a loving God? It may be that we like drama and seek danger over our own well-being. We play for the right to say we've lived dangerously. But the thrill of danger leads us into a dry desert. We search and search for water, but there is none. Our souls are thirsty.

3

Rivers of Life

He who does not know his way to the sea
should take a river for his guide.
~ **Blaise Pascal**

God is like a mighty river. Who will swim against His tides or overcome His currents? The strongest must retreat in surrender. Yet that mighty river, even as it threatens danger, is a guide for those who seek the sea. It carries all its objects down its flowing stream, planting trees along riverbanks. Steady is its rumbling and quenching is its taste. The waters are sweet and satisfy the thirsty.

Every generation has its thirsts. Everyone thirsts for meaning, for love, and for wonder. Some thirst for power, for prestige, or for fame. But our greatest thirst is for water, living water. Our souls resist every imitation—nothing but God satisfies.

Some choose to invent false meanings, seek false loves, and wonder at small things. They are like travelers who've missed the main attraction. But why this dryness and death when God's river flows with life eternal? We have believed a lie; we must awaken our hearts to reason. We must change.

We must change, not only in our thinking but also in our believing. Our destinies are the outcome of what we believe about our place in the world. They are not fixed by circumstances or scripted in tragedy. God Himself is leading, working, and making us ready to seize our meaning, grasp our loveliness, and embrace His wonder in us. But will we let His river guide us? Will we let His waters satisfy us? The answer will determine our satisfaction.

God wants an answer. He waits to grow us in His watered land of righteousness where emptiness is overrun by streams of life. Yet, one moment after another, we search after other waters to quench us—we thirst in silence. Who will mend our breaking hearts and water our parched souls? Eternity is written in our hearts—earth's delights are never enough. The river of God is our reminder that something is missing. C.S. Lewis punctuated this problem when he said, "If I find in myself a need that nothing in this world can satisfy, the most probable explanation is that I was made for another world."[6] Yes, that's it. That is how we feel about ourselves and our desire to end our breathless desperation for something real. We want something to fill us, but nothing really does, so we're left grasping, like drowning men for straws. None of us ever fully escape this madness; we are all vulnerable to it. We're desperate.

Children are free from the desperation that we grownups are so familiar with. They see everything with simplicity. Going past my neighbor's house one day, I could not help but stop and listen to the screams and joys of their four little children. Such delight and innocence made me long again for my childhood, if only for a moment. Children have little worry and simple faith. That may be the reason Jesus called upon a child to settle a debate between two grown apostles: *"Who is the greatest in the kingdom of heaven?"* they asked. In the next verse, we read these words: *"And calling to him a child, he put him in the midst of them and said, 'Truly, I say to you, unless you turn and become like children, you will never enter the kingdom of heaven'"* (Matthew 18:1–3 ESV). The vital lesson taught to us by children is the elusive act of believing. In this parable, Jesus identified a lack of simple faith as the core to our shortsightedness and waywardness. We seem to think that children believe with simple faith because they don't know any better. Jesus said it was the opposite of what we thought it to be. Jesus contradicts us all the time. His logic is counterintuitive to our logic.

In the very next verse, Jesus said, *"Whoever humbles himself like this child is the greatest in the kingdom of heaven"* (Matthew 8:4). He was defining "greatest" as it pertains to faith, not to accreditation, achievement, or entitlement. There were many in Jesus' day, as there are today, who need to hear this message and rethink their definitions. Neither titles nor achievements, not even the applause of men, can make one great. The

kingdom of God is spiritual, and children see with
their hearts. We must believe it before we can understand it. Children possess the ability to admit their
need. When they hunger or thirst, they cry and are
fed. As adults, however, when we hunger or thirst, we
try to fill ourselves with other things. We are masters
at avoiding the cries of our hearts.

Children grow up eventually and become like us,
sadly. They go to school and experience the world we've
handed them. They witness hate and jealousy and
exhibit racial prejudice. They feel heartbreak and loss.
Philosopher Blaise Pascal reminds us: "The Christians'
God is a God who makes the soul aware that He is its
sole good: that in Him alone can it find peace; that
only in loving Him can it find joy."⁷ The knowledge
that nothing but God can satisfy our deepest longings
should serve as motivation to keep God at the center
of all our seeking.

But we ignore the thirst within us and resist with
passion what is best for us. In return, we discover that
no scale can measure the pain that weighs upon hearts
made for God. Still, God is infinitely patient; He calls
us forth from our desolation. Our desolate and lonely
hearts can quickly find refreshment; the river of God
awaits. It fills our longing for deep springs of life.

LIVING WATERS

Rivers play a major role in the life and sustenance
of most, if not all, civilizations. The thirst for rivers
of life is as ancient as time. Genesis 2:10 tells us, *"A*

river flowed out of Eden to water the garden, and there it divided and became four rivers" (ESV). It took four verses to describe this river, but only one verse (Genesis 2:7) accounts for the creation of man. There is common agreement that this river could be a spring that came from the ground or a tall mountain stream that flowed down to the garden. Once the river reached the center of the garden, it divided itself into what would become four huge rivers. This would necessitate a huge garden. But could there be a hidden message in these verses? Could this river be allegorical for God's ability to refresh and satisfy Adam and Eve? We cannot be sure of this from a single chapter in Genesis, but we can draw some interesting assertions from the prominent use of the word *river* in Scripture.

In Psalms 36:8, for example, *river* is used in describing God's blessings: *"They feast on the abundance of your house; you give them drink from your river of your delights"* (ESV). Psalm 46:4 says, *"There is a river whose streams make glad the city of God"* (ESV). The prophet Isaiah gave God's promise to His people, saying: *"I will extend peace to her like a river, and the wealth of nations like a flooding stream; you will nurse and be carried on her arm and dandled on her knees"* (Isaiah 66:12 NIV). Finally, in the closing chapter of Revelation, we read these words: *"Then he showed me a river of the water of life, clear as crystal, coming from the throne of God and of the Lamb"* (Revelation 22:1 NASB).

It is clear from these verses, and many others throughout the Bible, that the word *river* plays a vital role in the history of God's redemption. Could it be that the architecture of Eden revealed God's case that only He could satisfy? Think about that for a moment. I do not mean to hyperbolize or dramatize what some might see simply as part of the account of creation and nothing more. Yet who can contend that God is a God of mystery? My simple question is this: What if God was saying something about His ability to quench through the fixture of this river in Eden? It certainly would not be the only time or place He used His artistry to convey His character. Psalm 19:1–2 tell us, *"The heavens declare the glory of God, and the sky above proclaims his handiwork. Day to day pours out speech, and night to night pours out knowledge"* (ESV). Here again is another instance where God's creative work calls His subjects to take notice, to watch and be amazed. How easily we ignore God when He speaks.

Jesus understood this tendency in us. He punctuated this message in a conversation with a woman from Samaria who came to Jacob's well to draw water. Jesus spoke these words to her, as recorded in John 4:13–14: *"Everyone who drinks of this water will be thirsty again, but whoever drinks of the water that I will give him will never be thirsty again. The water that I will give him will become in him a spring of water welling up to eternal life."* It does not surprise us to hear her response in verse 15: *"Sir, give me this water, so that I will not be thirsty or have to come here to draw water"* (ESV). She got the message loud and clear.

Like most of us, this woman had a need that nothing or no one could satisfy. She had tried to meet that need through many illicit relationships that left her more broken with every encounter. The day she encountered Jesus was a new beginning. Her spiritual roots were starving for something real, and her spiritual leaves were dry. In that single encounter, her entire life was transplanted to new and fertile ground where dryness had no reach. That is the story of God. That is the picture of redemption. That is what happens when dying trees encounter the river of God. Jesus said, *"The water that I will give him will become in him a well of water springing up to eternal life"* (John 4:14 NASB). These are not vain words. Jesus knew our ability to look right past living water on our way down the desolate road to waters that do not satisfy. How many throughout history have made that journey? How many more will no doubt follow? Regrettably, we are blind to things that matter. We are prone to enjoy empty thrills and ignore fountains of living water for a dry desert of sinful pleasure.

AN ACHING SOUL

Even the wisest person falls prey to the trap of empty pleasure. Outside of Adam and Eve, Solomon proved that better than anyone. His life tells the most compelling story of a man who, despite his great wisdom, could not change, at least not until his life was almost over. He lived a thrilling yet empty adventure of regret. The thing with Solomon was not that he tried and failed in his quest, but that he exceeded the efforts of anyone before him to discover enjoyment. It is as if he did not know how to change course and stop his descent into misery—he wondered off course to an early death.

But what do we know about Solomon's life? What made him so susceptible to the drifting balloon of pleasure? The answer may be closer to home than you might imagine. Poet Henry David Thoreau helps us understand this problem. He wrote: "Time is but the stream I go fishing in. I drink at it, but while I drink, I see the sandy bottom and detect how shallow it is. Its thin current slides away, but eternity remains." The thin currents of pleasure never last, do they? They slipped away from Solomon, leaving him in dismay.

Solomon had creative instincts and a great propensity for danger. He is like all of us in that regard—we are all intrigued by danger. This is no small matter. Despite Solomon's wisdom and wealth, the need for danger was knocking down his sacred heart with intense fury. The louder the knock, the greater his heart began to ache, wondering, wishing, longing. What was so furious about this knocking? To answer that question, we must reopen a chapter of Solomon's life and discover the clues he left us. In them we find not only the pathology of an aching heart, but also warnings to resist his path and learn from his lessons. This begins with a prayer. It's a prayer that Solomon prayed with intense honesty. 1 Kings 3:6–9 records Solomon's earnest prayer:

Then Solomon said, "You have shown great lovingkindness to Your servant David my father, according as he walked before You in truth and righteousness and uprightness of heart toward You; and You have reserved for him this great loving-kindness, that You have given him a son to sit on his throne, as it is this day. Now, O LORD my God, You have made Your servant king in place of my father David, yet I am but a little child; I do not know how to go out or come in. Your servant is in the midst of Your people which You have chosen, a great people who are too many to be numbered or counted. So give Your servant an understanding heart to judge Your people to discern between good and evil. For who is able to judge this great people of Yours?" (NASB)

There is little doubt that Solomon was motivated by an undying devotion to the God of his father David. In verse 6, he elevated the God of David, recognizing all of David's blessings as a reward from God Himself. Because David walked with God in truth and an upright heart, he was called not only a man after God's heart, but also a man in whom his son Solomon recognized the work of God. Again, in verses 7 and 8, Solomon came before God with sincere humility. This is the kind of brokenness that helped make his father David a mighty warrior. Now Solomon was going to become king over Israel, and he turned to the God of his father by whose strength alone he would succeed.

The words of his prayer are a powerful display of affection and devotion to God.

As it turned out, because Solomon asked for wisdom and not wealth, God gave him wisdom as well as more wealth and power than anyone before or after him could boast. But something strange was going on within the walls of Solomon's great palaces. The man who had been given so much simply wanted more. Why was he not satisfied? Imagine having palaces, servants, gardens, and every kind of material blessing. That would make many people happy, but for how long? All the blessings in Solomon's life made him more of a danger to himself. Instead of seeking the God who brought him wealth, he was seeking wealth without godly direction. As a consequence, his heart began to ache. He was broken and filled with regret. Ecclesiastes 1:2 discloses the lessons and pains that Solomon was made to bear because of his wandering: *"'Vanity of vanities,' says the Preacher; 'vanity of vanities, all is vanity'"* (NASB).

The wisdom that once guided him he called futile. The pleasure that once filled him would become a great burden, a threat to his soul and life. Labor was once Solomon's delight, but after looking back, he would find little joy in it. In a shocking confession, he admitted to hating life itself. It is incredible how far he had fallen from the life he once imagined. He was deceived.

By the time Solomon was ready to leave the world, he had known more pain than he thought imaginable. But Solomon left us his lessons. In the final chapter of Ecclesiastes, he told us what life is all about: *"The conclusion, when all has been heard, is: fear God and keep His commandments, because this applies to every person"* (Ecclesiastes 12:13 NASB). On the road to seeking God, something had gone bad for Solomon. He began his journey as a well-watered life but found himself in a dry desert, staggering from the burns of pleasure, thirsting for a land where God was gardener. To fully grasp the detour of Solomon, one must answer a pivotal question: Why would a wise man betray his God, compromising his life and honor for a graveyard of sin? What could have gone so wrong?

BETWEEN LOVE AND ACTION

Contemplating God's beauty should cause us to imagine nothing greater than God Himself. But in Solomon's case, as was true for Adam and Eve, a strange thing happened between his godly reflections and his actions. None of us would even dare to question Solomon's undying love for God. Yet none of us can avoid the tragedy we find in his story of mistaken loyalties, obsessive longings, and drowning passions. How does a man who loved God fail so terribly? Solomon allowed his heart to be infiltrated by desires contrary to what he believed and knew to be true. His beliefs and actions were at war. Fleshly desires soon took over his godly longings, pitting his knowledge against his emotions. In his heart, he wanted to do what God commanded, but like all of us, he lacked the ability to do what he knew was right.

Here I think is a tremendous truth worthy of our attention. The reason we fall so short of what we know to be right is due to a lack of emotional satisfaction with God as the *Summon Bonum*—the ultimate good thing. But this raises other searching questions: How did Solomon not know where this would lead? Where was all his wisdom in these vital moments? The same questions must be asked of ourselves, lest we forget our own contradictions. The heart is easily habituated to strange loves.

The most well-established truth in human affairs is human sinfulness. We can't go too far before admitting this. We know that all the great men of the Bible, and indeed throughout history, have tended to fall to some vice or contradiction. What, if any, explanation can we offer as the cause of their failures? Why do we lose all rationality when sin appears at our door? We want what we want, and often God's way and our wants are irreconcilable, even at the cost of losing ourselves. That is the great shame of our humanity. We leave our lamps behind because we love darkness. We empty our water cups because we seek euphoria, not quenching. But euphoria never lasts. Like Adam and Solomon, we wink at God's call to obedience, ignoring the fact that we do so at the cost of exchanging His cup of innocence for the leaking cup of regret. If I am honest about this, really honest, I have to confess that I sometimes don't know what I want. Do I want God, or do I want my twisted image of gold? Do I want righteousness or something like it that lacks any true demands?

Paul described his own struggle with sin (Romans 7) and mirrored the horror Solomon felt as he sat in his bed of regret: *"I hate that part of myself that brings me into alliance with sin,"* Paul said. I feel that way, don't you? Here lies the great conflict of our humanity. We love the good we do but fail so often. We hate the evil we do but can't seem to bring an end to it. We're seeking a way out of that tension but fall right back into it.

LOSS OF INNOCENCE

Life is full of many firsts—a baby's first tooth, a child's first steps, a teenager's first date, and a young person's first broken heart. That's the way it goes in this hasty quest to grow up, fall in love, and live happily ever after. That is the dream that is gifted to us from childhood. And we are dutiful in living our fantasy as best we can. The only trouble is that life is not a fantasy. One thing is clear about us: We don't like to be normal. That's boring. So we journey on, seeking drama and trying to assuage the contradiction we feel in our hearts. But like everything else, time shatters all our illusions and makes it painfully clear that our innocence is lost. We discover that with all its beauty, this world is also a place of inescapable sadness. Everyone feels this weight, but only a few ever get close enough to see their part in the ordeal. Like Adam and Eve, we miss it. Like Solomon, we miss it. Like the heroes, kings, and peasants of every era, we look past the stubborn reality that God is the only remedy.

Adam and Eve made a choice in believing that God was hiding something from them, only to realize that God was protecting their innocence. Now that they acquired knowledge, were they asking for their innocence back? They learned, as we all have, that God is hiding nothing. *Hiding* is what we sinners do to mask our guilt, regret, and shame. God does not hide good things from us. But when innocence is lost, there is nothing to do but hide. We are masters of this art. We hide by faking a smile and drowning our nights with drinks or drugs or anything else that keeps us from pain. Solomon did so too. He learned that vice, as do we, from Adam.

We also have those moments of greatness that we chronicle in pictures, stories, and memories. We like being reminded of these victories, and we like showing them off to others. They shape the way we see ourselves and the world. In them, we recall moments of our innocence. But all of that is blown away by vicious winds of time. This weighs on our soul too, as we realize that not even our best victories restore the grandness for which we were created.

Our failures keep reminding us of what we've lost. Although separated from us by time, such memories remain alive in our hearts to remind us of where we've been. But if we let them, they can also remind us that the sum of our lives always includes the future. As a young man, I learned that four things never come back: the spoken word, the spent arrow, the past life, and the neglected opportunity. This maxim explains the basic challenge we face, to get it right the first time—to keep our innocence. But we all fall down. That's life; we all drop the ball.

But nothing is ever completely lost in the redemptive garden of God. He takes pleasure in the lives of His redeemed ones and makes all things new. Adam and Eve, as well as Solomon and everyone else who has ever lost innocence, know all too well the long reach of God's hand of grace. Who came looking for Adam and Eve after their rendezvous with the serpent? Who came looking for Cain after the murder of his brother Abel? Who came looking for Abraham, Moses, and Jacob? What about Solomon? The answer is God. The entire history of mankind is filled with examples of God recovering humanity from its incessant flirtation with sin and its reckless consequences. And still, despite His outstretched hands, we walk past God and invent other solutions to our basic need for aliveness. Becoming like God in both character and conduct is the meaning of true innocence. But we have to admit our terrible lack of it if we ever hope to live our best lives. We know that something is wrong, but we like to pretend everything is okay. We play games.

At the age of sixteen, I remember falling off my skates in the presence of the girl who had captured my imagination. I got up with a bruised knee and deep elbow wounds and was able to walk off like a movie star. I spent the rest of the week recovering at home, but at least I showed grit in the moment. I thought it would be better to endure the pain than to seem weak and act hurt. Silly, I know. Why did I pretend in order to impress? I was acting out of ignorance and blinding pride. But where did all this come from? Where did we learn to act this way? The answer lies under the debris of the ancient Garden of Eden, the birthplace of every human vice and every evil under heaven. Solomon himself reminds us, *"There is nothing new under the sun"* (Ecclesiastes 1:9 NIV).

All human sins are traceable—they are inherited from the ancient gene pool of Adam and Eve. Any attempt to explain this by another means is the best explanation of the problem itself: by denying our genetic relationship to Adam, we end up proving it. If we are not sinners, then why are we sinning? Our aliveness and meaning depend on our desire to become people who are innocent of great transgression and able to live freely, from the heart. Bondage and freedom are enemies that cannot coexist in the same heart. Freedom is like a river of life bringing rest to hearts who delight in God's commandments. A restless heart, on the other hand, is breeding ground for bondage.

4

Prisons of the Heart

*If you can just say exactly what has you imprisoned,
the doors spring open.*
~ **David Whyte**

I t was the day of offerings, a time to give from the
heart. Two men would present their offerings, most
likely for the first time. One would be accepted and the
other rejected. The story in the making is a tragic but
true story of how one man's heart was taken captive by
jealousy, hate, anger, and pride.

Cain looked on with interest as God received Abel's
sacrifice. He must have waited eagerly for his turn. But
God was looking at his heart and saw a problem—a
heart made for love was giving way to rebellion, threatening to imprison him. Cain's very heart was on the
line—a target for imprisonment. His twisted thoughts
would soon lead to deadly anger and the shedding
of innocent blood, its stains not easily washed away.
What began inside the chambers of his heart grew into
devious feelings that would lead him to murder. Cain
deceived himself by acting against his own interests.

He permitted jealousy, hate, anger, and pride to take root in his heart, turning a brother into a killer.

A JEALOUS RAGE

Adam must have been overjoyed and Eve bursting with delight at the birth of their first two sons and everything they dreamed for them. What little we know of Cain and Abel is left mostly to the imagination. The evidence of their character is revealed by their names and actions. Cain's name means "spear," and he worked the ground. Abel's name means "a breath," and he was a keeper of sheep. Abel's sacrifice had found favor with God, but Cain's was rejected. Both men brought something from their industry: *"In the course of time Cain brought to the LORD an offering of the fruit of the ground, and Abel also brought of the firstborn of his flock and of the fat portions. And the LORD had regard for Abel and his offering, but for Cain and his offering he had no regard. So Cain was very angry, and his face fell"* (Genesis 4:3–5 ESV).

Many have argued that God's rationale for accepting one man's offering and rejecting the other had to do with their offering. Although I do not intend to resolve this debate, something about this strikes me as odd. If both offerings were equal in value, then why was one rejected? The problem appears to be not in the offering but in the heart of the one presenting it. As we have already seen, something about Cain's heart was at odds with God. The proof is in his response to God's open invitation to change. In Genesis 4:7, we read: *"If you do well, will you not be accepted? And if you do not do well, sin is crouching at your door. Its desire is contrary to you, but you must rule over it.*" Cain's attitude gives us reason to believe that he was bent on avenging his dignity after the rejected offering. But the door was wide open, and God would accept him when he was acceptable. Cain was not acceptable; as a consequence, nothing he brought would be accepted. He needed a changed heart. In the verses that followed, we find out that sin not only crouched at Cain's door, but it also ruled his heart and would soon undo his life.

While they were away in the field, Cain rose up against his brother and killed him. The door of grace was open to him, yet he chose to walk into the closing door of jealousy, a prison from which he would not soon escape. When God asked about the whereabouts of his brother, Cain responded, *"Am I my brother's keeper?"* (Genesis 4:9). That is the question of a hardened man. God did not ask Cain if he was his brother's keeper; he only asked him where his brother was. In his answer, Cain revealed his character. Just like Adam and Eve, Cain was attempting to hide from God. It did not work for them and it would not work for Cain. The man had lost his heart.

Cain could not control his rage, and it led him down a regrettable path of violence. He chose to kill rather than listen to the voice of warning. He chose to save face over being good before God, even taking matters into his own hands. To him, nothing mattered except his need to justify himself, and in so doing, he reduced his brother into an object and a hindrance in his way. That's what jealousy does: it causes one to reduce another. It demeans.

A man of violence who lives by his sadistic and twisted notions is a coward who belongs in the dungeon he has made for himself. Such was God's verdict in the accounts before us: *"And now you are cursed from the ground, which has opened its mouth to receive your brother's blood from your hand. When you work the ground, it shall no longer yield to you its strength. You shall be a fugitive and a wanderer in the earth"* (Genesis 4:11–12). These are gripping words from the mouth of God about the first biological seed of His creation (Adam and Eve were made from the dust), reckoning to Cain His justice.

None of us can escape the long and unrelenting reach of God's justice; all the deeds of the flesh will be judged. Cain, along with anyone who chooses rebellion over submission and who mistakes violence for justice, will face the fiercest justice of all—eternal separation from God. Rebels can seem like heroes, but in the end, they are on a lonely road to defeat and isolation, for God's face is set against those who resist His way.

The door of God's mercy swings open in every direction, but so does His justice. None of us should forget this lesson; we are human, mortals who must one day face our Creator. God keeps the books. This should not be the only motivation to do right, but it must not be forgotten. Our key motivation must be the antithesis of Cain's answer. We must learn to be *our brother's keeper.* That is the work we should aspire to as God's children.

Cain is mentioned in two other instances in the Bible outside of Genesis. Both cases connote negativity, reflecting a model of wrongdoing. His is not a model for any generation, including ours. His sin was duplicitous and dangerous, and the consequences were tragic. What was wrong with Cain? In search of an answer, we discover some telling words from the Apostle John as he describes what godliness is not: *"Do not be like Cain, who belonged to the evil one and murdered his brother. And why did he murder him? Because his own actions were evil and his brother's were righteous"* (1 John 3:12 NIV). Here, the apostle recognizes Cain in no flattering fashion; he calls him an evil man. Cain's heart was bent in opposition to God, and his thinking was shaped by ungodly rebellion. He killed his brother because of jealousy. He was willing to live with evil, and yet he wanted a righteous reward and God's acceptance. Amazing, is it not? In an effort to tolerate himself, Cain removed a good man from his presence. Humanity continues to repeat this folly. The truth is that we will never discover peace in warring hearts. We can have no lasting peace until we stop insisting on making our brokenness work. We like to pretend that our brokenness is wholeness; it is not.

Cain killed his brother because Abel was a righteous man whose life offended his own evil heart. God calls Cain an evil man. None of us should wish such words as our legacy. Cain had gone terribly wrong. The

Apostle Jude joins this commentary, and he warns us to avoid what he called "the way of Cain." In Jude 11, he cautions, *"Woe to them! For they walked in the way of Cain and abandoned themselves for the sake of gain to Balaam's error and perished in Korah's rebellion"* (ESV). If a man is judged by the company he keeps, Cain found himself in a notorious gang of evildoers of the highest order. He is mentioned with two other rebels: Balaam, a prophet for hire who wanted the better of two worlds but ended up losing them both; and Korah, Moses' antagonist who led a rebellion against God's servant and was buried alive with his evil posse in the wilderness. These men all have in common a dangerous tendency to establish their own order and ignore God's authority.

God must not be ignored when he speaks or resisted when he commands. Too many fugitives have wandered the earth since Cain, searching for a peace they lost to their rebellious hearts. They forget that peace is not something that finds us; it's something we create by our actions.

God loudly warned the Hebrews, *"You shall not covet"* (Exodus 20:17 ESV). God's desire is that we are most satisfied with Him. This is reflected in the words of the first and second commandments, in which God warns of having no other god before Him or any image of His likeness anywhere in His universe. God goes on to offer this justification: *"You shall not bow down to them or serve them, for I the LORD your God am jealous God"* (Exodus 20:5 ESV). You may be asking, why does God justify His jealousy but condemns it in His creation? Jealousy in God is justified because He wants what's good for us. God Himself is what's good for us, and He is therefore morally obliged to confer on us this goodness.

God is the only indestructible reality in the universe. He is holy and eternal. "Holy" means that He is in a league of His own, separated from the sin, injustice, hate, and evil of the carnal order. Nothing can be compared to Him because nothing is like Him. To what do you compare a being who is fully love, infinitely holy, completely just, absolutely mighty, perfectly benevolent, wholly eternal, genuinely unchanging, and truly all-powerful? God has no beginning or end. Such honor can be ascribed to nothing and no one else. Such a being must not only want the best for His creation, but He must also be the best guarantor of his subject's cries for satisfaction and meaning. God is jealous because He can afford to be. He lacks nothing.

A God who lacks nothing must already have everything. Having everything allows Him to be what we need in abundance. Jealousy in God elevates our need for all that He is; jealousy in us reveals our terrible inadequacies. Cain became a jealous man when he embarked on a mission to protect his self-importance. Violence became his means of achieving what should have been procured through obedience to his Maker. His jealousy morphed quickly into anger.

THE FACE OF ANGER

Everything about a person can be deduced by looking at the face. A smiling face most likely means the person is happy. A blank face means one is distracted or disconnected. A sad face conveys sadness or grief. Our faces say everything we're feeling, thinking, even wishing. Anger also has a face. If ever there was a man whose face exhibited anger, Cain would be that man. So angry was he that not even God could calm him down. Cain had ample time to calm down, but his reaction showed that he was unwilling to see what he was becoming. In Genesis 4:6–7, we hear God pleading: *"Then the LORD said to Cain, 'Why are you angry? And why has your countenance fallen? If you do well, will not your countenance be lifted up? And if you do not do well, sin is crouching at your door; and its desire is for you, but you must master it'"* (NASB). The tragic truth from Eden until today is that we have not mastered it. Mastering sin; who can achieve this feat? Why would God even ask us to strive to master sin? Is that realistic? If not, what is God saying here? To understand this, you have to look beyond the call itself to the nature of the God in question.

The heart of God is an eternal flame, a fiery pool of godly desire for our good. Nothing consumes me more than the idea that God loves me so much that He pleads with me to overcome my wayward, sinful impulses. God wants Himself for me, just as He wanted Himself for Cain. The problem with anger is it makes us strangers from ourselves. Have you ever seen someone really angry? It's ugly. Cain was wearing that face, and God was graciously pleading with him to put on the face of love. We all have that choice, don't we? We can take on the face of anger and be like our enemy or take on the face of love and be like our Maker. Sadly, Cain fell for the former. He became more like his enemy, Satan. Let us also look at our own faces lest our secret feelings, angry stares, and hidden passions lead us where they led Cain.

In such moments, we lose ourselves like sheep in the company of roaring lions or like a warrior without his vest, breastplate, and sword. We become a vulnerable target for the enemy of our souls. But we must never forget whose we are. Dietrich Bonhoeffer, a young theologian who became a threat to Adolph Hitler, captured the weight we all carry in search of ourselves amidst the deep questions of our hearts. From his jail cell, he wrote with the stinging bite of realism that should compel us all to stop and listen:

Who am I? They often tell me
I stepped from my cell's confinement
Calmly, cheerfully, firmly,
Like a squire from his country-house.
Who am I? They often tell me
I used to speak to my warders
Freely and friendly and clearly,
As though it were mine to command.
Who am I? They also tell me

I bore the days of misfortune
Equally, smilingly, proudly,
Like one accustomed to win.
Am I then really all that which other men tell of?
Or am I only what I myself know of myself?
Restless and longing and sick, like a bird in a
    cage,
Struggling for breath, as though hands were
compressing my throat,
Yearning for colors, for flowers, for the voices of
    birds,
Thirsting for words of kindness, for
    neighborliness,
Tossing in expectation of great events,
Powerlessly trembling for friends at an infinite
    distance,
Weary and empty at praying, at thinking, at
    making,
Faint, and ready to say farewell to it all?
Who am I? This or the other?
Am I one person today and tomorrow another?
Am I both at once? A hypocrite before others,
And before myself a contemptibly woebegone
    weakling?
Or is something within me still like a beaten
    army,
Fleeing in disorder from victory already
    achieved?

Who am I? They mock me, these lonely questions
 of mine.
Whoever I am, thou knowest, O God, I am
 Thine![8]

Bonhoeffer's lonely questions are not so unique. They were also Cain's questions. Beneath his raging face of anger was a hurting man, longing for a place in his Maker's heart. *What is my place in this world? Where do I fit in this beauty around me? What is my part in a game where others exceed me? Will my best be good enough?* Such were Cain's questions, pounding in like a mighty sea. God came to his tumultuous heart with words smooth enough to calm his anger: *"Why are you angry? And why has your countenance fallen? If you do well, will not your countenance be lifted up? And if you do not do well, sin is crouching at your door; and its desire is for you, but you must master it"* (Genesis 4:6–7 NASB). Can you hear the voice of a loving God in these words? Can you hear God's longing for Cain's good? We may never know the love God has for us unless we look upon Him and feel the gentle breeze of His eternal love. That love alone has the power to replace anger. Like a wayward son who despises and casts his face from his father's love, so Cain walked away, one lonely step after another. He mistook strong love for harsh rejection and covered his face with anger. In shame, he went his way.

We forget that despite all that is amiss with us, we are creatures of a loving God who wants us for Himself. Nothing is therefore lost in the grand design of God for us, His children. But the lurking danger of anger hangs in front of us. It displaces us from our place before a loving God. It makes us doubt His intentions and goodness, shifting our gaze to the sinful faces of others, and worst of all, ourselves. If Cain only knew that he was loved, wanted, and sought after with great urgency, he would have refused the face of anger. But his anger resisted both reason and love. And without reason and love, we are like wild beasts devoid of understanding.

THE IRONY OF HATE

Murder is not so hard when hate controls the heart. Hate is like a drug; it sets one up to believe the unbelievable and do the unthinkable. Hate had grown so deeply into Cain's heart that he disregarded what God called sacred. He believed so much in himself that the interests of others were of no concern to him. He would have his way, no matter who paid the price. Centuries later, Jesus prescribed an antidote: *"You shall love your neighbor as yourself"* (Matthew 22:39 NASB).

The single most important insight into this love is that it is simultaneously God-generated and self-re-producing. Anyone who has experienced love must necessarily give it back. Love should not and cannot be contained. *"If someone says, 'I love God,' and hates his brother, he is a liar; for the one who does not love his brother whom he has seen, cannot love God whom he has not seen"* (1 John 4:20 NASB). The idea is that love and hate are incompatible, everywhere and in every situation. In other words, if you truly love God, you will also truly love your brother. There can be no exception. The universe in all its dimension, complexity, and design is but the overflow of God's love. Only a loving God can create a universe in which love cries out over everything. Love is the language of God. It flows from one circuit of the earth to another, and nothing escapes it. But as it is with everything else, the enemy of God tries to stifle God's loving expressions. His weapon of choice is hate.

What does it take to hate someone so much as to want him dead? Mind you, it's one thing to tell someone to drop dead and quite another to take his life by bloody ambush. That's what happened here. With stunning horror and shock, God uttered the words, *"Cain rose up against Abel his brother and killed him"* (Genesis 4:8 NASB). All of heaven stood still when Abel's body hit the ground. Cain lured his brother to a place where no one would see, where he could conceal his crime. But who was he fooling? Did he believe he could cover up his crime before the eyes of God? Cain convinced himself that his cover-up was a smashing success—before God showed up, that is. *"Where is your brother Abel?"* God asked in Genesis 4:9 (NIV). He was in essence only reading the verdict to Cain, not seeking evidence to indict him. God does that to show us how far we've gone off the deep end and to offer us a chance to repent.

God is omniscient. Nothing is hidden from His presence:

Where can I go from Your Spirit?
Or where can I flee from Your presence?
If I ascend to heaven, You are there;
If I make my bed in Sheol, behold, You are there.
If I take the wings of the dawn,
If I dwell in the remotest part of the sea,
Even there Your hand will lead me,
And Your right hand will lay hold of me.
If I say, "Surely the darkness will overwhelm me,
And the light around me will be night,"
Even the darkness is not dark to You,
And the night is as bright as the day.
Darkness and light are alike to You.
      (Psalm 139:7–12 NASB*)*

Cain discovered that truth that day, as do all of us who dabble in the playground of sin. Killing his brother threatened God's sacred order. With Abel's death, the second act of sin's rampage was complete. Adam and Eve fulfilled the first act by taking the fruit of which God said they should not eat. Here, Cain fulfilled God's promise to Adam: *"In the day that you eat from it* [the tree of the knowledge of good and evil] *you will surely die"* (Genesis 2:17 NASB). The peace of the Garden of Eden was a distant memory. In a once loving family, a brother murdered a brother.

Hate waits along every hidden path and highway; we are its targets and must guard against it. It works much like an aneurism. According to mediLex-icon.com's medical dictionary, an aneurysm is: *"A circumscribed dilation of an artery or a cardiac chamber, in direct communication with the lumen, usually resulting from an acquired or congenital weakness of the wall of the artery or chamber."* The symptoms include nausea, vomiting, eyesight problems, seizures (fits), loss of consciousness, confusion, a drooping eyelid, a stiff neck, and light sensitivity. In much the same way, hate weakens the wall of the heart, resulting in spiritual nausea, confusion, and vision problems with all its vicious symptoms to follow.

Imagine what it must feel like to have all of these symptoms at once, operating on a spiritual dimension! It leaves one incapable of thinking or managing their emotions. Cain killed his brother because his heart was bleeding, which caused everything else to bleed with it. What intolerable sadness. A heart made for love was bleeding, dying right before the eyes of its Maker.

Think of the agony God felt for Cain and for anyone living with hate. Jealousy made Cain an architect of evil, anger disfigured his face, and hate left him bleeding. Standing before his dead brother in shock, Cain quickly realized that he was the one who was really dead. Here again lies the glaring irony of hate— the outcome it produces makes us worse than before, not better.

THE DREAM KILLER

We learned in the first chapter that curiosity is dangerous. We are about to learn that pride kills dreams. Cain had big dreams. He wanted to be larger than life, more luminous than the brightest star, all on his own. He failed to see that his grand dreams could never compare to God's dreams for him. *"Who is the man who fears the LORD? He will instruct him in the way he should choose. His soul will abide in prosperity, and his descendants will inherit the land"* (Psalm 25:12–13 NASB). God is a partner and a friend to all who seek His face and pursue His dreams. But God opposes those who despise Him. God's dreams for us are best. They come alive in us the moment we make Him the willful object of our devotion. *"Seek first the kingdom of God and His righteousness, and all these things will be added to you"* (Matthew 6:33 NASB). Cain was seeking his own kingdom, and like many after him, kingdoms crumble into the dust and rubble of history.

Pride sent Cain's dreams into a free fall. It is the engine to all other evils. Pride is easily shielded behind false motives and illustrious visions. But if you look past the poses, what you find is a sick imposter. Words from an Air Supply song, "Making Love Out of Nothing At All," capture this imposter in all of us:

> *I know just how to whisper.*
> *And I know just how to cry.*
> *I know just where to find the answers.*
> *And I know just how to lie.*
>
> *I know just how to fake it,*
> *And I know just how to scheme.*

I know just when to face the truth,
And then I know just when to dream.

Nothing is as true to me as the reality that I am a man of complex and contradicting impulses. At times I feel big, larger than the stars of heaven, confident and alive in ways that I think would make God proud. But what is that to me? I can be so impressed with myself that I forget who the credit belongs to. Then I hate that part of myself that embezzles God's honor, and I vow with *humble* resoluteness never again to sell God's glory. Then I do it again. Listen to the words of the prophet Jeremiah: *"The heart is more deceitful than all else and is desperately sick; who can understand it?"* (Jeremiah 17:9 NASB). He is right. That's who we are: deceitful and desperately sick. Who will come to our rescue and bring an end to our masquerade?

The question at the end of the verse is pivotal to resolving that conflict we all feel within ourselves. He asked, *"Who can understand it?"* But do we ever want to hear the answer to the question? Can we not listen for just a while to the one who created the heart and has the prescription for its illness? God, the Creator and lover of our souls, speaks in Jeremiah 17:10: *"I, the LORD, search the heart, I test the mind, even to give to each man according to his ways, according to the results of his deeds"* (NASB). God is the judge, and He warns us that there is a cost to pride. Its ripples reach far and wide across centuries and cultures, demonstrating the volatility and ignorance that has far too often entrapped us humans. Pride is a bogyman. It comes before all great disasters in the affairs of man. It harvests lives with impunity. Solomon reminds us, *"Pride goes before destruction, and a haughty spirit before a fall"* (Proverbs 16:18 ESV). The sacred testimony of Scripture and that of human history judges him correctly.

Solomon is saying that pride is an ambush of the soul, a force against our desire to choose what is good. This truth underscores the need to guard our hearts. I am convinced that the greatest responsibility of any human is to have a heart that is free from imprisonment, guarded against faulty deliberations and fixed against false delights. *"God resists the proud, but gives grace to the humble"* (James 4:6 NKJV). God came to Cain at the first murder scene of history and offered him a chance at repentance. In Genesis 4:6, the Lord asked, *"Why are you angry? And why has your countenance fallen?"* (NASB). This was Cain's opportunity to put aside his pride and seize the moment of grace. But as we know from our Sunday school lessons, Cain resisted with reckless indifference.

As younger brothers do, I wanted to be like my big brother. He was good at sports, especially cricket. I was the less talented one, and it seemed that everyone reminded me of this. Did I ever get jealous that my brother was so often praised? My answer should not surprise you: yes, I was a bit jealous. But I was determined to make my mark and get my brother to pay attention. I knew I could never be a fast bowler like him, so I focused on fielding, and I eventually became good at it. In the process, I learned to congratulate others for their gifts while I continued to work on my own.

Once I learned that lesson, my brother was no longer my competition but my inspiration. Could it be that this is where Cain went wrong? What if he had seen his brother's triumph as a cause for celebration rather than a reason for jealousy? Pride leaves no room for congratulations.

In truth, pride is a hiding place for all the things we abhor about ourselves but wish for others to mistake for self-confidence. Cain demonstrates that the worse kind of pride is that which makes us believe our own delusions. Scripture reminds us, *"Rejoice with those who rejoice, weep with those who weep"* (Romans 12:15 ESV). Cain had that choice. But in choosing to be more like God's enemy, he sought good for himself and no one else. Cain was indeed his brother's keeper, but pride blinded him to that reality.

The news of Cain's actions was a bit too much for Adam and Eve. Jealousy mixed with hate, anger, and pride had now metastasized into full-blown murder. Cain had stiffened his neck against God and denied that he was his brother's keeper. God would give to him according to his deeds. Now Abel's blood was crying out to God from the ground, and God would hear his plea for justice. We must always remember that He is a God of justice and concedes nothing to evil. In Genesis 4:11, God turns to Cain: *"Now you are cursed from the ground, which has opened its mouth to receive your brother's blood from your hands"* (ESV).

Work would become more difficult for Cain. The ground would raise its voice against him as a witness to his unjust act of murder, an act that God pleaded with him to avoid. He did not listen and would now become a *wanderer* on the earth. Such is the fate of all who resist God. Then we hear these searching words from Cain's mouth: *"Cain said to the LORD, 'My punishment is too great to bear'"* (Genesis 4:13 NASB). Cain received his just deeds and agreed with God that His justice was right, but it was too difficult for him to bear. Cain became a walking target, a man without home or country. The awfulness of sin is not only what it does to us, but also what it does to the heart of our Maker. God was hurting over Cain's sin and anguish. How God wished that Cain had chosen humility before pride overtook him. We can be sure that God does not delight in punishment. He wanted many blessings for Cain just as He wants for all children of Adam. How God longs for us to listen and to surrender our wayward hearts and desperate thoughts. Millennia later, He still warns us to avoid Cain's indifference and its high cost.

Imagine Cain, head in hands, with tears pouring down his face and regret eating at his soul, wishing he could undo what he did. Listen to him reflect on the cost of his pride. *"Behold, You have driven me this day from the face of the ground; and from Your face I will be hidden"* (Genesis 4:14 NASB). Working the ground would be painful, but the loss of God's favor stalked him with deep regret. How he longed to be Cain again, the man his parents wished and hoped he would be, the man he was made to be. Pride imprisoned his soul and kept him from seeing the trap set for him. He willingly played in a sinister plot to undo his life.

Regrettably, we face the same temptation to construct our own reality outside of God's rule, to be our own bosses and chart our own course. It might not be murder, but the danger still lurks in our hearts. Jealousy blinds us, anger defaces us, hate bleeds us, and pride kills our dreams. This should send us scrambling to God, like birds from the hands of a fowler or like drowning men in search of rafts. His laws are meant to be a shield from pride's ambush. Any other route invites destruction, a price too high for us to pay.

5

The Law of the Lord

The law of the LORD is perfect, reviving the soul; the testimony of the LORD is sure, making wise the simple.
~ **King David (Psalm 19:7)**

Perfection is elusive. Despite the fact that we require it of others, we find it impossible to achieve it ourselves. Everyone around us plays a part in feigning perfection in public while painfully conceding the reality in private: *"All have sinned and fall short of the glory of God"* (Romans 3:23 ESV). Our best intentions fail us, and our long-held ideals elude us. We are the children of Adam. One only has to read the news, study history, or better yet, take a look within to behold the hidden darkness we foster. The evidence compels the conclusion that we are desperate and sick. We publicly talk of sacred things while we privately disavow them.

It is ironic how quickly we criticize other sinners while we are guilty of the same deeds. Are we not just like the law breakers? Didn't Jesus die for their forgiveness too? Apart from the daily grace of God, we would be exactly what we despise in others. The madness of pride is in our hearts; how easily we forget. What can ever truly free us, the lonely children of Adam? The perfect law of the Lord alone can revive and restore our wounded, hurting, and desperate hearts.

For as long as I can remember, I have had a soft spot for wounded things. I was eleven years old when I noticed from my house window a wounded bird hopping around, flopping helplessly to attempt what is usually done with ease. It was a yellow bird with a short tail and a broken wing. I ran to it with severe urgency, much like a paramedic to the scene of an accident. After chasing it through the yard for a while, I finally caught it. Like a patient doctor, I tied one leg with a short string and provided it with ripe bananas and water. More importantly, I washed its wounds with antiseptic liquid and added some special lotion to its wounds. This went on for at least four days. By that time, my patient, the yellow bird, was getting better. I planned to keep it longer for observation. (I have to admit that I had no idea what I was doing; I was modeling behavior exhibited by my mom, who often cleaned my many cuts and bruises from my childhood adventures.) One morning, I woke up to care for my patient, but it was gone. Someone had freed it.

I still remember the disappointment I felt because I did not have the chance to see my yellow bird fly to freedom. But the bird was free to fly. Every time I saw a yellow bird, I wondered if it could be my former patient. I would never know, but for what it was worth, I knew I saved that bird. In doing so, I learned a truth about humanity. Much like that bird, we are all wounded people, hopping and flopping around life. We need the attention of a diligent doctor whose love is stronger than our wounds.

David had his fair share of wounds, and he wrote both from the experience of those wounds and from the healing power of God's law. Listen to his words: *"The law of the LORD is perfect, restoring the soul; the testimony of the LORD is sure, making wise the simple. The precepts of the LORD are right, rejoicing the heart; the commandment of the LORD is pure, enlightening the eyes. The fear of the LORD is clean, enduring forever; the judgments of the LORD are true; they are righteous altogether"* (Psalm 19:7–9 NASB). Will you listen?

In these words, we find God's daring invitation to wounded people. Receive them and live; ignore them and face the horror of sin and its presumptuous path to death. God is calling our names in these verses. Can you hear yours? He is calling us to listen to wisdom and learn from it. Life is like an open window that shuts after dark. We don't have forever. In these six declarations, He offers us healing, wisdom, happiness, enlightenment, eternity, and justice. Let us try to unpack the treasures hidden therein, and by God's help, find the courage to apply them to our thinking and living. We will discover that God has good intentions for our lives that should make us giddy with delight. His law is not a burden. It carries away our burden.

SECOND CHANCES

When I was seventeen years old, I made it to the under-nineteen cricket team. You don't have to know anything about the game of cricket to understand that *I was giddy with excitement.* I remember being so excited that I could not sleep the night before our first big game. I had my white pants and white shirt ironed nicely, my shoes were in place, and I had a sense of anticipation that I can still recall to this day. I could not wait for game time. Taking my place at the crease and fully rehearsed, I was ready to save the day. Well, it did not go as I had rehearsed. I was caught at slips at the first ball. Slamming my bat to the ground, I walked away, head down and ego shattered in pieces.

But in cricket there are two innings, so I had one more chance at bat. As I prepared to face the bowler, I kept thinking how great it would be if I did well this time. The bowler moved in, and with one motion, I stroked the ball off my hips and down to the boundary for four—the umpire signaling in the affirmative. So began my rebound performance; I had redeemed myself from shame. You could not imagine the joy I felt in that moment. I can only describe it as a realization that I had risen out of a dark storm and into a glorious day of sunlight. I was restored. With one stroke, I went from shame to splendor. That's pure redemption. That's pure joy.

The psalmist David captured the same idea with these words: *"The law of the Lord is perfect, restoring the soul"* (Psalm 19:7). The law of the Lord gives us a second chance at bat. How many of us could refuse the chance to show our true stuff? We all want to redeem ourselves from past mistakes. No one goes on living with complete abandonment of the past—we all long for emancipation. Everyone suffering the shame of failure can stand upon this towering promise; the joy of restoration is not so far away. The perfect law of the Lord gives new life to our failed attempts, and dreams. It alone can lead us to the happy land of love where freedom is king.

A PURE HAPPY LOVE

It's hard to imagine anyone rejecting a second chance, but many do and suffer in silence behind their façades. One of the biggest façades we engineer is self-importance. People who live behind this lonely wall believe in themselves so much that they think others exist for their ends. Such people would collapse into chaos if not for their titles, honors, and past achievements. Their entire security rests on prefixes, suffixes, and pretenses. They fail to realize that their greatest joy is found in the One they belong to, not in what they do. Such people are a law to themselves. But contrary to this thinking, it is those who seek and love God's law who can know true freedom and experience true joy. This is the first step into God's pure love— to love His law. Christ commands us to love others as ourselves (Mark 12:31). That, above all else, is the mark of a person bestowed with the humility and fortitude to deserve *pure happy love*. What Jesus was saying is that until we can love others as we love ourselves, we cannot truly be free to live from the heart.

Listen to David's words: *"I run in the path of your commands, for you broadened my understanding"* (Psalm 119:32 NIV). Can you fix that image in your mind? David said that he would run as an athlete to the finish line—to God. What David said is simple. He wanted to run to God with urgency, readiness, and fervency. Is that how you see God's law? Many see it as restrictive and imprisoning. But not David. He continued, *"I will walk about in freedom, for I have sought out your precepts"* (v. 45). David did not view God's law with cynicism. He embraced it as a life-giving principle, a treasure to seek, and a gift to claim. People who live for their own honor are running from the law of God, not toward it. What do they gain? Misery. But those who run to God's law make great gain; they walk in freedom. If we want to live and walk in freedom, the message is simple: Run to God's law, for it is the key to wisdom. We cannot be truly happy without wisdom.

God knows our inability to use wisdom in living. It is for that reason that He reminds us, *"The testimony of the LORD is sure, making wise the simple"* (Psalm 19:7 NASB). You will notice two important concepts in this verse. First is God's trustworthiness. The word *testimony* is used when a witness is on the stand, telling the whole truth before the judge and jury. God reminds us that not a single word of His will fail to come true. If we plant our lives on His promises, we will reap a harvest of eternal life. Second, you will observe that

God describes us as *unskillful* or simple. Yes, you heard it right: God calls us unskillful. Shocking, isn't it? But think about it. Are we not unskillful? Yes, we are, if we are honest with ourselves. We lack the skills to live the lives we were made for. We were made to enjoy God's pure, happy love. But our lives are replete with failures. Should we go on thinking we can handle everything just fine?

God is portrayed in Scripture as a potter. He makes things come to life. Imagine a lump of clay sitting in unformed mess—that is how we are without God. The problem is that we don't realize it until His wisdom shapes our thinking. He has to make us wise so we will grasp the love He has for us. He takes us one lump of clay at a time and shapes us, giving us form and making us beautiful. When the process is complete, we are able to say, *"I praise you, for I am fearfully and wonderfully made. Wonderful are your works; my soul knows it very well"* (Psalm 139:14 ESV). Until we grasp the intention and generosity of our Maker, we go on thinking we have a better idea of who we are and how we're meant to live. By His creativity, God makes us both willing and capable of experiencing His love and loving Him in return. This makes both God and us happy as we enjoy His fellowship and He our loveliness. Once we understand this, we want to follow His designs, and *simple* does not seem so offensive. We discover that God's greatest delight is seeing us thrive.

THE SEEING HEART

The heart goes to places where nothing else can. Its lenses are eternal. It sees deeper than telescopes. In his famous collection of thoughts called *Pensées*, Blaise Pascal (1623–1662) offered this pointed comment: *"Le coeur a ses raisons que la raison ne connait point."* It's translated, *"The heart has its reasons that reason knows nothing about."* That strikes me as not only true, but also pointedly jolting. He was right. The heart is pulled toward God in whom it finds meaning. Now we know why God spent so much time talking to us about the heart. One such example is in Psalm 19, which we've been exploring: *"The precepts of the LORD are right, rejoicing the heart; the commandment of the LORD is pure, enlightening the eyes"* (v. 8 ESV). The word *right* conveys the idea of a straight line. God's precepts or teachings are drawn with a straight line; they are without fault. They rejoice the heart because the heart thrives through righteousness—it sees best through God's eyes.

"The law of the LORD is perfect, reviving the soul; the testimony of the LORD is sure, making wise the simple; the precepts of the LORD are right, rejoicing the heart; the commandment of the LORD is pure, enlightening the eyes" (Psalm 19:7–8 ESV). These two verses must be taken together. They are connected by two important words. We've already been introduced to the word *right*. The next word is *pure*. It means without alloy or corruption. What a great, but lost idea! God's commandments and teachings are without crookedness and

corruption—they are exactly how they should be. They affect us in two ways. First, God's testimony delights the heart—it makes the heart glad. But His commandments take us further: they enlighten the eyes.

This is a colossal idea. God's commandments put eyes on our hearts. Do you understand what's happening in these verses? God's commandments will literally clean up the blinders this world has imposed on our sight. We live in a world of twisted thinking and false promises. We don't know who to trust because our enemies and our friends are often the same people, leaving us cynical about relationships. God's testimony and commandments will always be the truth. We will never have a reason to doubt the trustworthiness of our most important friendship—the one with our Maker. We have a straight and uncorrupted Maker who wants the best for us, who forgives us when we fall short, and who never spills our secrets! What does He have to gain? Our hearts.

God knows the value of our hearts. It's what He cares about the most. Psalm 19 is a declaration of God's love and delight for His created beings. He is saying, "Look what I have made just for your eyes and heart to see and love." In verses 1–6, He calls all creation to pay attention to the majestic works of His hands:

> *The heavens declare the glory of God, and the sky above proclaims his handiwork. Day to day pours out speech, and night to night reveals knowledge. There is no speech, nor are there words, whose*

voice is not heard. Their voice goes out through all the earth, and their words to the end of the world. In them he has set a tent for the sun, which comes out like a bridegroom leaving his chamber, and, like a strong man, runs its course with joy. Its rising is from the end of the heavens, and its circuit to the end of them, and there is nothing hidden from its heat.

It is as if God were calling on us to be in wonder of Him, to behold Him, and to be amazed. It's a romantic thing. That should not surprise us. Where did we get our idea of romance, anyway? We got it from God in whose image we are created. Don't let this surprise you; God is the original romantic. In verses 7–10, He continues to seek romance with us, this time through His written letters: *"The law of the LORD is perfect, reviving the soul; the testimony of the LORD is sure, making wise the simple; the precepts of the LORD are right, rejoicing the heart; the commandment of the LORD is pure, enlightening the eyes; the fear of the LORD is clean, enduring forever; the rules of the LORD are true, and righteous altogether. More to be desired are they than gold, even much fine gold; sweeter also than honey and drippings of the honeycomb"* (ESV).

When I was a sixteen-year-old boy, I enjoyed writing letters. I had several pen pals from different places in the Caribbean. But one particular girl grabbed my interest beyond that of any other. She was from Guyana, and although I never met her in person,

I was fond of her and even believed I was in love with her. We exchanged photos and shared our dreams and wishes to travel and to see the world. But chiefly, we wrote about ourselves. I fully intended to fly to Guyana to meet her, but I did not have the money. I eventually left home for the United States, and our communication ended. I kept her letters as a reminder and witness of where the heart could go through words alone.

I think God is doing the same thing in Psalm 19. He sent us His letters in the form of statutes and commandments. They rejoice our hearts and enlighten our eyes. What magic. That's the way it's meant to be. Our hearts are made for rejoicing, and our eyes are made to be enlightened. God is the letter writer whose words flow with ease and grace, painting images in our minds and leaving us astonished about who He is and what He wants for us. Would you take the time to recapture the magic with your Creator and read His letters? They will rejoice your heart and enlighten your eyes. Many of us have forgotten what it feels like to have a delighted heart and an enlightened eye because we've been seeking our own remedies.

GOOD MEDICINE

Solomon's search for pleasure left him damaged and in need of healing. We are like him in that regard. We need good, strong medicine for our wounds. Jeremiah also recognized the wounds of so many of God's people when he asked: *"Is there no balm in Gilead? Is there no physician there? Why then has not*

the health of the daughter of my people been restored?"
(Jeremiah 8:22 ESV). His question has been answered
definitively. God has the medicine for our wounded
hearts, but we humans love to find our own way and
prescribe our own treatment. We want to get the credit.
That's the trouble with us. We try to explain God by
constructing ideals from our vain imaginations rather
than the mind of God, and in so doing, we invent our
own solutions. Such invention exposes good men to
bad religion and confuses the laws of men for the laws
of God. The result is neither a better kind of man nor a
better kind of religion, just more religion and less love.

Nowhere is this more obvious than in the hypocrisy of the Pharisees of Jesus' day. It explains why Jesus
reserved his harshest criticism for their elite, calling
them vipers. Jesus reserved His fury for them because
they had taken words that were never said by God and
sold them as truth. Ruling from these dogmas, they
made themselves king, and God's truth became their
servant. Such is the sickness of manmade religion.
Pure religion, religion from above, is God helping
man become what he was made for. Man was made
to know God and to glorify Him. Any religion that
does not seek the knowledge and glory of God as its
only aim has diverted from God's law to serve its own
twisted fascinations.

The most popular religions are those that teach that
we have the power to define our lives, mark our boundaries, and decide our destiny. The creed of manmade
religion is taking from God what we want and giving

nothing in return. Our obedience is His greatest delight, and yet we resist with outright stubbornness. We are wired to resist God's will. We prefer to take our chances, even if they lead us down a dangerous and uncertain path to nowhere. Our arrogance is stunning. Or may I say foolish? How easily we fall to our own devices. We are not as wise as we think we are. Listen to God's commentary on our intelligence: *"For the wisdom of this world is folly with God. For it is written, 'He catches the wise in their craftiness'"* (1 Corinthians 3:19 ESV). We get caught with our hands in the cookie jar, and yet we do it again and again. Why?

Millennia after the Eden disaster, the Apostle Paul addressed certain philosophers in Athens (Acts 17:21–28) whom he managed to impress with his *new teaching*. In verse 21, we learn: *"The Athenians and the foreigners who lived there would spend their time in nothing except telling or hearing something new."* These thinkers got their pleasure in intellectual stimulation, and they spent enormous amounts of time imagining and inventing new ideas. They lived in a constant search of new topics upon which to think and give consideration. They expected no less from Paul, but as you will see, Paul had other ideas. After making a robust case for God's rightful worship, he added these words: *"'In him we live and move and have our being'; as even some of your own poets have said, 'For we are indeed his offspring'"* (v. 28 ESV).

Paul's response offers three solutions for our twisted imagination:

1. *In him we live.* This presumes that:
    a. Whatever longing we have has come from God;
    b. The essence of life is God Himself; and
    c. God must be the recipient of all our works.
2. *In him we move.* God is the generating force behind everything we do. He has given us all our capacities, intuitions, and abilities.
3. *In him we have our being.* To have *our being* in God is to be indebted to Him.

What better way to demonstrate our indebtedness than to fear God?

Returning now to the Psalmist, we read, *"The fear of the LORD is clean, enduring forever; the rules of the LORD are true, and righteous altogether"* (Psalm 19:9 ESV). It is by showing that we fear God that we learn how to love men: *"The fear of the LORD is the beginning of wisdom; all those who practice it have a good understanding. His praise endures forever"* (Psalm 111:10 ESV). We persist in ignorance, because when we operate outside the boundaries of God's law, we have no anchor.

God is God, and we are earthly creatures creeping through the narrow window of time. The fear of God is good medicine; it awakens us from the stupor of pride. Until we have a healthy dose of reverence for the Almighty and a conscious awareness of His nature, we live alone. Anyone who pays attention to God's work in creation, especially to the human body and its inexplicability, cannot help but be amazed. Yes, we are

God's design, fashioned to reflect His glory. We run on God!

But like it or not, we are stained by original sin. We cannot deny that it is written on our hearts. It plays out in the news flashes of violence around the globe; in the twisted ideology of terrorism and hate; and in the silent suffering of orphans and children in the grip of hunger, abuse, war, and sexual slavery. It rings out on the battlefields where war ravages cities and kills the innocent. It shouts on Wall Street where greed and ambition threaten the retirements of hard-working people, exposing them to an uncertain future. It sounds in the halls of Congress where the drive for power has left too many trails of corruption. Look what we've done. We have lost our footing. Will we recover?

God has more to add to our sordid and sinful achievements. Listen to how He describes us: *"And since they did not see fit to acknowledge God, God gave them up to a debased mind to do what ought not to be done. They were filled with all manner of unrighteousness, evil, covetousness, malice. They are full of envy, murder, strife, deceit, maliciousness. They are gossips, slanderers, haters of God, insolent, haughty, boastful, inventors of evil, disobedient to parents, foolish, faithless, heartless, ruthless. Though they know God's righteous decree that those who practice such things deserve to die, they not only do them but give approval to those who practice them"* (Romans 1:28–32 ESV). God's indictment is without ambiguity. Those who fail to acknowledge and fear God do so at a great cost. Without the fear of God, any number of viruses will enter the operating system of our hearts and make us vulnerable to the ugliness of which we are all capable. God is calling us to listen, and listen we must.

"They are more desirable than gold, yes, than much fine gold; sweeter also than honey and the drippings of the honeycomb" (Psalm 19:10 NASB). God's law is to be treasured above gold, diamond, rubies, and any other precious stone.

People today rob banks and break into homes to steal gold and diamonds. Wars are waged over precious stone and minerals in Africa and other places. Men use diamonds by the millions around the world to say, "I love you." The purest gold and the most expensive diamond fall miserably short of the intrinsic value of the law of God. Its ability to bring true joy and freedom is without comparison, and its taste is like the dripping of honey.

Growing up in Dominica gave me a chance to taste some of life's most delicious things. I grew up enjoying jelly nuts, fresh guavas, delectable oranges, fresh passion fruit, and sweet mangoes. On my way to our garden, I was invited by my cousin to see his honey hive. Tentative at first, I gave in to the invitation and watched as he extracted layers and layers of honey from his hives. Then he did the incredible—he cut me a chunk of honey. "Try it," he said. I tried it and promptly begged for more. I still remember the taste it left in my mouth as it dripped down my chin. I licked every last bit of that honey. That sweet enjoyment is

what is offered to those who love God's law. We can
lick our chins with delight and find rich healing and
enjoyment for our souls.

6

Waking Up Human

Human beings cling to their delicious tyrannies
and to their exquisite nonsense,
till death stares them in the face.
~ **Sydney Smith**

We are but a breath, a wind, a passing flame, but we pretend to be alive before the world. God sees us privately mourning the lives we wish we had, and He mourns too. He weeps over our pathetic attempts to live in our power and seek our own way. One moment, we are worthy of applause; the next moment, we are hiding behind our shame. One moment, we are lovers; the next moment, we are haters. One moment, we are optimists; the next moment, we are pessimists. One moment, we are saints; the next moment, we are sinners. That's what we are, isn't it?

We talk about love, yet we spew forth words of prejudice. We falsely judge and dismiss those who don't look, think, or act as we do. Then, in our attempt to incubate ourselves, we join *fraternities* and *sororities* (Latin words *frater* and *soror* mean "brother" and "sister") to foster our self-importance. This, along with other exclusive memberships, secret organizations, and private clubs blind us to the need to be our brother's or sister's keeper. But our desire for social significance must never be separate from our duty to manifest God's love. Failing to manifest love makes us internal, tribal, narcissistic, and completely opposed to God's nature.

We begin to view God as our own personal deity, a reflection of our gender, race, and political ideology. The manifestation of such false thinking distorts our view of the transcendent God who reveals Himself in all men. We forget that the God of the Bible is not white with blue eyes, as depicted in many paintings. Nor is He black with a goatee. He is not formed in the image of anything in heaven or on earth or under the earth. God is not conceived by human imagination or reduced to reason. Nothing can be ascribed to Him that He does not already possess. Who, then, is God, and how can we rightly relate to each other as those who bear His image?

A LOST IDEA

We come into this world and depart from it in much the same way. Both the beginning and the end of our lives may happen in a hospital. It can be said further that hospitals and graveyards are inevitable meeting grounds for us. But during our middle years of life, we seem to ignore this very biting reality. It is likely that at birth and at death, we have no prejudice. So why can't we live the in-between years with that recognition? Children enjoy each other with no thought for their racial, cultural, or economic status. If only we could all stay that way.

Imagine two people of different races and experiences who are both dying. They lie near each other on lonely hospital beds. Separated only by a colored curtain and a few breaths, they are both on the gliding path to eternity where they will face their Maker. Both men believed in God, but one is the son of slave owners; the other is the son of slaves. They lived their entire lives as enemies, but now, in their final moments, they have a chance to right the wrongs that divided them. What might two men in their predicament say to each other? What should they say?

Reason would suggest they begin with *reflection*. This is a lost word in the dictionary of modern man. We seem to reflect mostly on ourselves and whatever we deem necessary to achieve our own ends. But while reflection begins within, it never ends there. Reflection or *reflexio* means an "act of bending back," from the Latin word *reflectere*. It means "the bending or folding back of a part upon itself."[10] For our purposes, such bending back is not for blame, but rather for self-examination and correction.

If the men dying in adjacent hospital beds reflected on their lives, they would bend back in protest of how they lived. We have a word for that: *regret*. Regret means that if given the chance, we would do things differently. And people who regret tend also to repent. Repent means to turn or bend away from past sins. It is the best indication that one is serious about reconciling. Our dying men would achieve reconciliation if they could reflect, regret, and repent. It's a beautiful possibility when we rediscover the lost idea of reflection.

But in the segregated South, where these two men lived, they could not attend the same school, ride on the same bus, eat in the same restaurant, or even use the same restroom. The son of the slave has a painful memory; he carries the marks of his struggle. He remembers stories of their inhumane treatment; his wounds are still fresh. They won't let him forget. He lost his father by the hands of hate, and his brother's blood still cries out from the streets of protest. They see themselves through the prism of their history, but they are in fact more similar than they were made to believe.

In *Genetic Similarity Theory: Beyond Kin Selection*, researchers found: "A gene ensures its own survival by acting so as to bring about the reproduction of *any* organism in which copies of itself are to be found. Rather than behaving altruistically only toward kin, organisms are able to detect other genetically similar organisms and to exhibit favoritism and protective behavior toward these 'strangers,' as well as toward their own relatives. In order to pursue this general strategy, an organism must, in effect, be able to detect copies of its genes in other organisms. We order several data sets with this theory including (a) kin recognition studies in animals raised apart, (b) assortative mating, (c) intrafamilial relations, (d) human friendship and altruism, and (e) ethnic nepotism."[11]

Other studies, such as the Genome Project, conducted in April of 1983, confirmed that the three billion base pairs of genetic letters in humans were 99.9 percent identical in every person. Said differently, all humans are 99.9 similar and only 0.1 percent dissimilar. Taken together with the Genetic Similarity Theory and our own intuitive knowledge of our common identity, no one should be surprised to hear that we are cut from the same cloth. But sadly, we allow the 0.1 percent difference to come between our 99.9 percent similarities. These studies demonstrate: (1) we are cut from the same lump, (2) we are travelers on the same adventure, and (3) we are seeking the same destiny. Not only is it true that we are our brother's keeper, but we are also attached to the same human cord. Our survival depends upon each other.

Jesus spoke these words more than two thousand years ago: *"But I say unto you, Love your enemies, bless them that curse you, do good to them that hate you, and pray for them which despitefully use you, and persecute you; that ye may be the children of your Father which is in heaven: for he maketh his sun to rise on the evil and on the good, and sendeth rain on the just and on the unjust"* (Matthew 5:44–45 KJV). Did you not hear that God commands us to love our enemies? The command of Jesus is that we love what He loves without regard to accidental issues such as race, station in life, or previous history. In this rests the boldness of the Christian vision, that we must love our friends and enemies. With these daring words, Jesus reversed the entire history of our need to justify prejudice. He says to love each other without condition.

We must understand that until we adjust our thinking toward the command of love, we increase hostility. Our two dying men can choose friendship or expand their history of hate. They can leave the world more united or more divided. The same power is in our grasp too; may it not slip away. Loving each other is the best manifestation of what God is like. There is no greater healing than to love. *"By this all men will know that you are My disciples, if you have love for one another"* (John 13:35 NASB).

BROKEN BRIDGES

One hot summer afternoon, I wandered aimlessly in a desperate search for nourishment. *I could eat a horse*, I thought. Ahead was a Greek restaurant I had previously visited. I stopped in to place my order. Tired, hungry, and absent of patience, I intended to satisfy my hunger, nothing more. But something unexpected happened.

The man I took for nothing more than a worker at a restaurant welcomed me with a smile and followed it up with a beautiful surprise. "So what do you do?" he asked.

Drawn by his friendliness, I obliged. "I am a pastor, and you?"

His answer left me guilty about my own tendency to prejudge others. He was a former professor in the field of microbiology. Suddenly, the restaurant owner became an interesting party with whom I wanted to have a meaningful conversation. What was wrong with me?

Why did I decide the man had value only after finding out he was a professor? Why did I pre-judge him because he owned and operated a restaurant? We went on to have a wonderful conversation about life, philosophy, Greek culture, and my long-held desire to visit Greece one day. After our conversation ended, I left the restaurant feeling overtaken by guilt and a nagging sense of my own prejudice. I was distraught over my own sinfulness and pride. Then reason flew to me, taking me to rest safely in the splendid field of human possibility.

How easily we deny ourselves the chance to discover friendship. Why did it matter that this man didn't fit my profile? And why, in heaven's name, do I have a profile? God forbid that our friends don't share our race, class, or experience. What about the person who pumps our gas? How about the cashier at the grocery store? How about the flight attendant, the man with tattoos, or the smoker? Are they disqualified from our friendship because of their titles or stations in life? Do they not come from the same human cloth? Are they not on the same journey as we are? Are they not seeking the same destiny?

Our destinies are hinged by life, death, and eternity. This small window of time is our chance to build relationships with love and sweat and courage. We aren't bound by this, but rather, we are liberated by it.

The moment we begin to embrace the power of friendships, we realize that the obstacles and heartaches are worth all the trouble. We must desire to love others the way God does. If we are to love people, we must first be lovers of God. Jesus taught us how to form unlikely friendships. His model is simple and yet uncomfortable. We must take a risk on others.

A man's greatest treasure is the gift of good friends, and friendships always entail some risk. Remember, Jesus took a risk in loving us. He risked being rejected by us, and He was. Yet He died for our sake. People who take these risks also seem to have the space and capacity to give and sacrifice for others. Are you such a person? One of the most compelling passages in the Bible says, *"Greater love has no one than this, that someone lay down his life for his friends"* (John 15:13 ESV). In the audience that day was a tax collector whose name was Matthew. He had little in common with Jesus. He belonged to one of the despised classes, yet he became part of the inner circle of Jesus, the Savior of the world. You know him today as the author of the first book of the New Testament. Matthew's unlikely friendship with Jesus placed him at a strategic place as a witness to the life of the Messiah. Jesus' disciples took notice of how He lived and loved. He taught them. He laughed with them. He wept with them and washed their feet. Then, in intimate friendship, He died for them.

After His resurrection, Jesus' message was taken to the ends of the earth for many compelling reasons. First, He had demonstrated by signs and wonders that

He was God. By this I mean He performed miracles that no one else had done or could do, such as walking on water. Second, He lived a sinless life and preached a message that was impossible to ignore. Third, He rose again from the dead, affirming His deity. But one of the reasons these men were so bold in telling the story of Jesus was because of their friendship. This was not blind allegiance, for these men saw the entire story. They watched Him for three years and were amazed by His miracles. His friendship, however, compelled them to leave their homes, occupations, family, and country to tell the story of their carpenter friend who was the Son of God, the Savior in human flesh.

Jesus connected His life story with unlikely men and women who then told His story to the world. He showed us how one life can affect another, even when one is the Savior and the other a sinner. Remember the woman in Luke 7:35? One moment she was defying her body, degrading her own humanity, and the next she was washing Jesus' feet. Such unlikely people contributed to the story of Jesus. And He gave them life through friendship. In the end, they are forever tied to Jesus through friendship that led to redemption. That should turn our hearts upside down.

Every human being has equal value before God and man. No, the Founding Fathers of America did not make up that idea; it's an unambiguous declaration of God's purpose for humanity. This truth was also the driving force behind the Civil Rights Movement and other campaigns for social justice throughout the world. We may have formalized legislation that outlaws apartheid, segregation, and discrimination, but hate still rules our impulses.

Where hate rages, the bridge of love is broken. It was evident in the racial divide between Jews and Samaritans in the Bible. It is true of blacks and whites in South Africa and America, and it's prominent in the struggle between Protestants and Catholics in Ireland and between Turkish immigrants and German nationals. It festers in the rivalries between the Maori people in New Zealand and those of British decent, and I saw it with my own eyes in the Caribbean between Carib Indians and those of African descent. Prejudice is ugly.

It is into this darkness that Jesus came to be a friend who lights the way for sinners. He built a bridge for reconciliation and called it love. He did not leave us with a topic to be debated or discussed. His command was for us to *"Love one another as I have loved you"* (John 15:12 esv). Must we wait until life's final moments to learn this lesson? We have waited much too long. The gates are wide open; a table is set for the reconciliation God seeks. Who will join Him?

THE FLAG OF GRACE

Marcus Aurelius was a man of much influence. He was the emperor of Rome and a philosopher of the first order. In his *Reflections*, he wrote: "Fit yourself into accord with the things in which your portion has been cast, and love the men among whom your lot has fallen, but love them truly."[12] His words are still as luminous for us today as they were so many centuries ago. Aurelius reminds us that to resist each other is to resist both God and ourselves. We are more isolated, more wounded, and more empty when we fail to see in others what God sees in us. An unsatisfied life provokes a man to fight over things that secure neither his redemption nor his satisfaction. In fact, they make him a prisoner to himself. Until our hearts are saturated by love, they wage war against us and threaten to destroy us before our own eyes.

But before we can live up to Aurelius' lofty idea, we must embrace our humanity. This is a work of humility that opens us to ourselves with utter honesty. It says we are better, more human, and more alive when we live in unity with our Maker's intentions for us. Out of this freedom, we are compelled to take off our outer clothing of pride and love others without barriers. Jesus mastered this art. He was comfortable in the company of children, scholars, sinners, and saints alike. Nothing was too low or too meager for Jesus to do. He had nothing to prove, no ego to protect, and no image to uphold. He washed His disciples' feet. Jesus was able to love without limit and live without fear. *He always did what pleased the Father.*

So many of us walk around trying to prove that we are this or that because we do not know who or what we are. Before we become capable of serving others, we must understand what God intends for us. Jesus is not promoting a doctrine of tolerance or nicety. He is commanding us to love deeply and genuinely from a free and spacious heart, touched by love. And this love tends to surprise us; it reaches past our darkness.

Some of the greatest men in history have left us mystified by the tragic trails they leave behind. Kings, presidents, politicians, poets, artists, and peasants all fall by the same vices. They are victims of a tragedy that stretches all the way back to Eden. One such person was John Newton. As a sailor, Newton participated in the business of slave trading, profiting off the backs of innocent human beings taken by force and sold into slavery. His dehumanization of other human beings was taking a toll on his conscience.

On a stormed-tossed sea, with his ship on the brink of wrecking, John Newton gave his life to Jesus after reading Thomas à Kempis' *Imitations of Christ*. After his conversion, he was promoted to captain and continued in the slave business until he could no longer reconcile his faith and his life. At age 82, Newton said, "My memory is nearly gone, but I remember two things, that I am a great sinner, and that Christ is a great Savior." What a stunning confession! Our hope is that a better world awaits those who seek Christ through forgiveness and grace. Before long, this same slave trader and mutilator of human innocence became the man we remember for the most well-known hymn of any age: "Amazing Grace, how sweet the sound, that saved a wretch like me. I once was lost, but now I am found, was blind but now I see."

Have you ever watched a june bug struggle in the sun? One afternoon, I saw a multi-colored bug on its back, struggling to flip itself over. Its tiny insect legs moved furiously, trying to gain footing. It stopped for a minute, all worn out, appearing to be finished. It had given up and would soon die in the hot sun, for it could not do what needed to be done. I decided I had to intercede. I took a stick from the garden and gently flipped it off its back. It thanked me by flying away with its glorious colors shimmering in the sun. We are like that june bug. I will always remember the impact it left on my own sense of need for Christ. We cannot do for ourselves what is necessary to live freely. Who will see us struggling and allow us to live? God stands over us with His long stick of love. He waits for us to admit our weakness and look to Him for mercy and help.

The moment we throw our hands in the air, love rushes to our rescue. It frees us in mind, soul, and body as we run into God's spacious garden and taste His freedom. Newton's confession teaches us that without the grace of Christ, we will do the unimaginable.

By the time John Newton left this world, he was a man fully restored. On his tombstone are found these words: "John Newton, Clerk, once an infidel and libertine, a merchant of slaves in Africa, was, by the rich mercy of our Lord and Savior Jesus Christ, preserved, restored, pardoned, and appointed to preach the faith he had long labored to destroy." If we allow the grace of Jesus in, He will break the barriers that keep us from loving others as He commanded. The human heart is deceitful enough to create both its own loves and its own enemies. When that happens, God erects His flag of grace upon our hearts.

UNTIL WARS CEASE

There will come a day when fighting will end. We humans have caused each other so much pain, but one day we will wake up glorified. Heaven will bring an end to all of our nonsense. But God's gift of eternal life is for the present and for all eternity. Eternal life is not some fatalistic dream of rescue after a lifetime of misery. We live with misery because we choose to. We choose to live under the spell of our fallen nature and not our heavenly one. We are creatures of God, ordained for greatness and endowed with His divine powers. He has given us all things for life and godliness through His knowledge, virtue, and excellence. The idea of heaven is within our hearts; it is the promise of life with God and our fellowmen. It is present, but we must grasp it before it slips away.

On Christmas Eve 1914, in the midst of World War I, men who were tired of decimating each other entered into an unlikely pact. As depicted in the movie *Joyeux Noel*, we catch a glimpse of the hope for peace within us all. On that evening, Scottish, German, and French soldiers engaged each other from their trenches through a chorus of carols and music, chocolates and champagne. As enemies of war, they killed each other, but through a game of soccer and an exchange of pictures of their wives and children, they were able to imagine a bold new world. Against all reason, they forged an unlikely bond. In the midst of war, they reclaimed their humanity and realized the possibility of peace through war. To match other moments in history, unfortunately, they returned to violence.

Imagine the challenge of returning to war against the father of the child whose picture made you smile. Imagine killing a father whose love for his son spills out from the photos, letters, and stories you've heard. Sadly for these men, they had to return to the ugly side of their nature. Their ceasefire was a momentary victory and represented a desire for peace and harmony that we all share. It was a glimpse of the glory we humans were designed to reflect. But like them, we also return to our battles as heaven weeps over us.

We are capable of great evil, but we must never forget that we are created in the image of our Maker. The novelist Agatha Christie said, "One is left with the horrible feeling now that war settles nothing; that to win a war is as disastrous as to lose one."[13] She was right. No one wins when we butcher each other in cold blood in the futile quest for peace. We all agonize over this conflict between war and peace. We look with disgust over what we've done. Blood is on our hands, and we cannot escape the thick drops that have stained our innocence. Where can we look to find ourselves again? Do we have any hope of ever washing away the guilt? There is a remedy; there is a cure. The *fountain filled with blood, drawn from Emmanuel's veins* still cleanses the guilty sinner who plunges beneath that flood. He washes white all who dip themselves into His crimson flow. We need His cleansing.

The stains of sin have touched every man and woman, from Eden to this day. We have wasted our lives with senseless tyrannies that enslave not only ourselves, but also those who inherit the hate we leave behind. They too must suffer the brutality of a world in the grip of human nonsense. Must we be proud of such ignominy? Our future awaits; it can be more of the same or more of what God in His love desires to achieve through us. *"He* [God] *will judge between the nations and will settle disputes for many peoples. They will beat their swords into plowshares and their spears into pruning hooks. Nation will not take up sword against nation, nor will they train for war anymore"* (Isaiah 2:4 NIV). And while our hearts wait for that day with eager desperation, the power to end all wars lies within us.

7

The War Within

Have patience with all things,
but chiefly have patience with yourself.
~ Saint Francis De Sales

Heaven is calling. You can hear its call, but you can't obey its command—you're in a dream, a paralysis. You try to move, but your body resists; your best efforts leave you trapped inside a battlefield of raging conflicts. Sound familiar? That's how it is inside this world of the human heart. Obstacles greet us daily; something is always standing in the way, rendering our best intentions useless. "Why is this so hard?" we ask. We stamp our heels in angry protest. What will end this constant war between our sacred longing and sinful fantasies? In this war, victory is tenuous but well worth the fight. Our hearts wait for repose, for all of the battles fought and defeats suffered by man throughout history have been the outcome of our greatest challenge: the war within.

Since Eden, our hearts have suffered defeat upon defeat. We are ravaged by the sickness of sin and its death grip on us. Its effects have left us exposed and vulnerable. We display grandiose contentment in public, but in private we suffer in anguish over the truth we know about ourselves. Simultaneously, we are worthy and unworthy, loving and unloving, believing and unbelieving. We are prisoners even in our freedom because we seek it within ourselves. Then we discover that broken people can neither achieve nor maintain true freedom. We need healing for our wounds. We need a warrior King who will fight for our hearts and lead us from the fields of battle to the streets of victory—a victory that has already been won.

REPEATED STRIKES

We are waking up to a world *still* at war as the forces of evil gather for a well-planned strike against our hearts. This is not the first time Satan has attacked this vital region of God's created masterpiece. It began long ago when two unassuming humans listened to the invitation of a lying serpent, and we suffered sin's first strike, forever losing our innocence. Our wounds trace as far back as the ancient Garden of Eden when we lost the crucial war for our hearts. But now, the vicious killing serpent has masked his plots and disguised his raging hate in other forms; his diabolical mission is to steal, kill, and destroy.

Most of us think of the devil as the fictional character depicted in children's plays, with eyes peering through a mask and his hand holding a pitchfork. In John chapter 10, Jesus described the nature of a good shepherd and that of one posing as a shepherd.

According to Jesus, Satan feeds God's sheep with delicious lies, seeking them out for revenge: *"The thief comes only to steal and kill and destroy"* (v. 10 NIV). Satan comes to take from God's children whatever brings God glory. His goal is to destroy and to render us worthless. That lack of understanding cost Adam and Eve their paradise and has cost us everything. The false shepherd is a vulture waiting to turn our hearts into lumps of dead flesh and to proclaim his triumph.

Satan has made his intentions clear: his mission is to take territory belonging to God and make it his. His battle begins and ends with the heart. If he could win even an inch of the heart, his goal would be achieved. We need to understand this. The battle between God and His enemy is not ideological; it's personal. He knows that whoever controls the heart also controls its destiny. He is fighting for the title and right to God's sacred property. The battle for the human heart began in Eden, but it's still raging.

Let us never forget that every human being since Adam and Eve enters a raging battlefield. We have all sustained various injuries. Our hearts have been infiltrated; they are divided, even broken in their deepest places. Through Satan's cunning lies, this brokenness is manifested in three key ways: he isolates us through rebellion, he punctures our family ties, and he ambushes us with legalism. All of this leaves us trapped in a wobbly circle of dissonance.

REBELLION'S ROAD

On a rainy Dominica day, I was shaking in my boots when a day of *would-be* crab catching left me standing alone in wet clothes, a bruised knee, and the approaching darkness of night. I had left that afternoon to hunt for crabs. Despite the warning of my mother, I took my large hanging bag, machete, and knee-high boots and was off on my mission. By the time I got to my hunting spot, it was getting dark, but that did not stop me. Off I went into isolated bushes where hardly anyone would go except on a rainy day like this. I had climbed to a great height a hundred feet above the main drag, approximately seven miles from home.

I made a good catch that day, and then I started to descend. That's when all hell broke loose. The rain became heavier, the skies became black, lightning was flashing through the sky, and the pounding rage of thunder could be heard for miles. In my hurry, I tripped over a rock, slammed my right knee, and rolled thirty feet—every bit of it in terror. Leaving my catch, I reached for my wounds, stumbled down a wet, slippery path, and called for help. There I was, standing in the pouring rain and darkness.

I cannot describe the isolation I felt that day and night, along with the fear of wondering if I would make it home. Standing in that darkness and feeling wet, hungry, and afraid made me realize the high cost of rebellion. I could not get past the awareness that on that long stretch of road, no one was there to help. I never want to feel that way again. Yet I walk down a similar road spiritually whenever I look past God's loving presence to embark on a silly adventure that always leaves me isolated. Everyone has felt this throbbing kind of isolation at some point.

We feel it in the silent cries of our wounded hearts. We feel it in our thirst and hunger that nothing in the world seems to satisfy. We feel it in our souls as they cry out for a higher reason and purpose for life along this broken trail. We feel it in the loud echoes of loneliness, fear, and death. We cannot shake the feeling that we were made for something more. That feeling, whatever we call it, is a reminder of what we're missing. We are standing in the rain; we are isolated. The greatest apostles, prophets, kings, and philosophers have all wrestled with this dilemma. They remind us that the war within is fierce, entrenched, and costly.

We must discover the truth of what we've lost— we have lost our chutzpah, or what others have called moxie. A part of the human soul is in hiding. We jeopardize our mission the moment we stand alone in rebellion's darkness. Paul described this in Romans 7:21–25: *"So I find this law at work: Although I want to do good, evil is right there with me. For in my inner being I delight in God's law; but I see another law at work in me, waging war against the law of my mind and making me a prisoner of the law of sin at work within me. What a wretched man I am! Who will rescue me from this body that is subject to death? Thanks be to God, who delivers me through Jesus Christ our Lord!"* (NIV).

Paul was admitting to a darkness in himself that hindered his ability to fight off the impulses that led him into rebellion. This rebellion had suppressed his true self, the real man who was created for freedom. Even when he wanted to do good, Paul found that rebellion took over. This is true of us too; we rebel and rationalize our sin, reason against reason, and become a law unto ourselves. As Paul found out, only Jesus was able to set him free and restore his unity with God and his sanity. He teaches that winning this war requires that we come out of the cave we're hiding in, recognize the limits of our humanity, and fall upon the grace of Jesus Christ. God's Son, with His power, will lead us as we march into the victory that awaits us.

Still, we must fight: *"Therefore put on the full armor of God, so that when the day of evil comes, you may be able to stand your ground, and after you have done everything, to stand. Stand firm then, with the belt of truth buckled around your waist, with the breastplate of righteousness in place, and with your feet fitted with the readiness that comes from the gospel of peace. In addition to all this, take up the shield of faith, with which you can extinguish all the flaming arrows of the evil one. Take the helmet of salvation and the sword of the Spirit, which is the word of God"* (Ephesians 6:13–17 NIV). Claiming our rightful place in the kingdom is not up to God; He has already enlisted us in His army of redeemed rebels. Will we wear His uniform?

But let us not forgot that wearing the uniform is not the essence of a soldier. A soldier has to fight. And in this fight for our souls, Satan concedes no ground. His mission is to undo our unity and freedom. He spares no lies, holds no punches, and withdraws no temptations until we're in total isolation. That's where he wanted Adam and Eve—on the run and afraid of their Maker's voice—and he is still banking on the chance that we've forgotten his evil tricks.

In the children's book *Tuck Everlasting*, author Natalie Babbitt tells the story of a young girl who faces the decision of returning to her legalistic parents or staying with a new family who offers a chance at freedom. As she ponders this wonderful new possibility, the text reads, "Closing the gate on her oldest fears as she had closed the gate of her own fenced yard, she discovered the wings she's always wished she had. And all at once she was elated. Where were the terrors she'd been told she should expect? She could not recognize them anywhere. The sweet earth opened out its wide four corners to her like the petals of a flower ready to be picked, and it shimmered with light and possibility until she was dizzy with it ... why, she, too, might live forever in this remarkable world she was only just discovering ... she ran shouting down the road, her arms flung out, making more noise than anybody."[14] That's the posture of God's sons and daughters. When we finally understand His boundless love for us, we fling our arms open in delight, forsaking the cold and isolated road of rebellion, and run to freedom. Once we do, none of the threatening terrors lurking outside our gate can restrain us.

FAMILY WOUNDS

If you enjoy children's books, you are sure to remember when Piglet sidled up to Pooh from behind:

"Pooh," he whispered.
"Yes, Piglet?" Pooh asked.
"Nothing," said Piglet, taking Pooh's paw, "I just wanted to be sure of you."

I have read more children's stories as an adult than I did as a child. Something about the tone and clarity of those simple stories helps me reflect on the common need we all share for love, friendship, and family.

Like Piglet, we have the need to be sure that we have someone to rely on. Without that solid sense of certainty, we grow up missing a part of ourselves. We need it from our parents, siblings, friends, cousins, and neighbors. But as I am finding out, the greatest deposit of that certainty comes from our fathers. In their absence, we are left wounded. How do I know this? I am a son who's been unintentionally wounded by his father.

I can now accept this cruel realization because I now have the courage of my heavenly Father. My earthly father and I have never hugged or cried together. He has never spoken the words "I love you" to my yearning ears. He missed all of my soccer and cricket games. I saw him once a month when my mom would send me to pick up child support for my brother, sister, and me.

I have never said a word to them about my pain; they are learning of it the way you are—in these pages.

My father set the stage for my life by *not being there.* That's how I felt for most of my young life. God was not a wellspring of affection and welcoming tenderness to me, for I had mistakenly viewed my heavenly Father through the experience of my earthly father. My story with God should not take you by surprise. There are many others like me; they carry their scars in silence inside a turbulent storm of fear and questions. I do not speak for them. I only remind you that they're out there. They hurt and they cry, sometimes in silence. Some may be crying now beneath the weight of *absence.*

All of our stories are as unique as snowflakes. We have all experienced hurt and rejection, causing us to become strangers to those we love and even to ourselves. One day, I met myself in an expected moment of honesty, and I knew I had to take action. I phoned my former pastor, and so began the rest of my life.

"Brother Charlie," I said, "I would like to talk to you about something."

He responded with the same generosity and care that I remembered. He is the finest servant of God that I know, the kind of man I want to be. "Briant," he said in his Southern accent, "I am going to pray that the Lord shows us where to go." His prayer began. He was just thanking God for making me sharp and wise when the phone cut out. I quickly called him back, but again our line went dead. We both recognized the urgency of our conversation. We both later agreed that spiritual forces were attempting to sabotage what God in His love wanted to achieve. I jumped into my car, drove out to the street, and found a parking spot alongside the road. There, with cars whizzing by, I found a place where the phone reception was adequate. We returned to the beginning of our conversation.

"Lord, please bring Briant to see the things you want him to see tonight," was his prayer. For a while, the whole thing appeared a bit juvenile, but I was about to be surprised by God.

My emotions began to unravel in a way I never saw coming. The wounds of my past were surfacing like an enormous object in still water. In a matter of moments, memories of my childhood came to me in haste and fury. They pierced my hardened exterior and showered pain upon my heart. *Why should I go there?* I wanted to know.

My heart was raging like a troubled sea. Snapshots of my early life were about to remind me of the place where my wounds began. They led me to a memory I had forgotten until that day. I was about eight or nine. My father, who had eleven children by five different women, was a distant man to me. I was sent to him to collect monthly child support. As a young child, I dreaded the task. On that day, I stood outside my father's house, gazing from the street, too afraid to come near. I stood outside, looking on as minutes merged into innocent sorrow.

Who should I blame for this wound? Should I blame my mom for sending me or my dad for making me too afraid of him to come freely and sit at his table? Should I blame both of them and God for allowing an innocent boy to experience such a haunting moment? My mom could never be blamed for any such thing, I decided. She was my angel. She was my father in a sense, with the absence of my dad. Therefore, I blamed God, but especially my father for causing me to stand outside his home, wishing I could know my own dad.

Many of the lingering issues of my life had their genesis in that moment of lost innocence. I say this both with tearful sadness and exhilarating joy—sadness because I shouldn't have had to face my own dad with fear, and joy because I am discovering the truth that God, my Abba, my Daddy, was always there, even in that moment, loving me. He is not to blame for that or any other moment throughout my life that brought me pain. In my ignorance I blamed Him, but I now praise Him.

God, the Father of this once frightened heart is in pursuit of other wounded children who stand outside the gate of their father's heart, who wonder about their place in this world, who struggle to find a shoulder for their tears. A true dad embraces the heart of his child. Children don't grow up emotionally healthy because their fathers buy them gifts or pay child support. Giving them a roof over their heads and food on the table will not do the trick either. Children develop safe, healthy, and free hearts when fathers spend time teaching them how to love, listening to their dreams, and inspiring a passion to change the world. They don't learn this on the streets or from friends. Education does very little to improve things. I did not rediscover my heart in seminary, church, or at a conference, and neither will this generation. I found my heart in brokenness before God.

Being vulnerable was never my cup of tea. Avoiding vulnerability is a common trait of wounded people, especially men. But as I discovered, until we accept our wounds, there can be no healing.

The day I began to listen to the voice within me while in complete stillness, I knew that intention could turn to action. When inner listening turned to an inner realization, I was ready to pour my heart out, even if I did not know how or what would come of it. I only knew it was time to be real. You may be hiding behind smiles while the inner sanctum of your heart bleeds. You know you're wounded, but you're too afraid to say it. I did and now confess that I am a grown man but still am a son in need of my Father. You are not too old to join me in discovering the joy of sonship, for God is *"a father to the fatherless"* (Psalm 68:5 NIV).

POLICING GRACE

I became a Christian when I was seventeen years old. My vocabulary of religious thought included hypocrite, backsliding, and a cluster of hollow axioms. I did not want to be a hypocrite. The way my mom said the word made it seem ugly. Backsliding struck me with a sense that if I ever did it, I would end up dead, maybe struck by lightning. I soon learned another word that made me boil—legalism. I have watched it damage good men, corrupt innocence, and become a terrible burden on the backs of well-meaning people.

I admit that I was nearly infected by this religious disease. Fortunately, I was released by grace and set free. This legalistic religion advertises perfection without love, holiness without examples, and moral virtue without moral struggle. It is for the have-it-together people who protect their righteous self-image behind a wall of secret sins and private despotism. They defend the claims of Jesus without the need to live them. They are ambassadors to lives they've portrayed but never actually lived. Such is the religion of the legalist, and they are as abundant as they are insidious.

Legalists hate transparency and stifle grace. People of this school attend glorious services, sit in pampered pews, sing in sanctimonious choirs, preach in golden pulpits, and theorize with glossy dictums and robust reasoning, but they stumble on grace. These *righteous ones* are the undeserving. They are sold on the fictional Scripture that Jesus came to save them—the righteous, the organized, and the well-educated. As it turns out, they are wrong about what's important and right about what is not. They have hijacked the message that Jesus came to deliver to us, the wounded sons and daughters of Adam.

Jesus regularly encountered unfriendly legalists of his day. In Matthew 15:1–3, we read: *"Then Pharisees and scribes came to Jesus from Jerusalem and said, 'Why do your disciples break the tradition of the elders? For they do not wash their hands when they eat.' He answered them, 'And why do you break the commandment of God for the sake of your tradition?'"* (ESV). I would have loved being there to witness that encounter. These men had the audacity to question Jesus' authority on a number of occasions. It is as if they saw themselves as His equal, having the chops rivaling a legal scholar.

In their minds, righteousness was about external things, such as paying tithes, reading and following the Law, and of course, washing hands. Jesus' question left them looking foolish: *"Why do you break God's commandment for the sake of your tradition?"* (Matthew 15:3 ESV). Jesus wanted to know why they were asserting their opinion over the commandments of God. I imagine Him turning to a Pharisee, pointing a finger, and delivering with an exclamation: "Hypocrite!"

Hypocrisy and legalism are joined at the hip. The word *legalism* is defined as "strict, literal, or excessive conformity to the law or to a religious or moral code."[15] And hypocrisy conveys the idea of an actor on stage, in character. His act, as it turns out, is not to be imitated at home. Those who would attempt to emulate this act should be on notice—life is not a play. Jesus saw them for what they really were, and hence, they incurred the wrath of an otherwise genial Messiah.

While the scribes and Pharisees were acting the part of righteousness on stage, they were not attempting it in the real world. To them Jesus declared: *"But whoever causes one of these little ones who believe in me to sin, it would be better for him to have a great millstone fastened around his neck and to be drowned in the depth of the sea"* (Matthew 18:6 ESV). How piercing. Can you hear God's dreadful threat to any who mislead God's children behind the dark curtain of legalism? Yet those who live behind this desperate wall believe so much in themselves that others, even God, exist only for their purposes. They pay little regard to the warnings of Scripture. They would collapse into chaos if not for their titles, honors, and achievements. Their entire security rests on prefixes, suffixes, and pretenses. The Pharisees had become a law to themselves, and Jesus was closing in on them for a big confrontation.

As recorded in Luke chapter 11, Jesus entered the house of a Pharisee and sat down for dinner. As dinner was served, the Pharisee noticed a not-so-flattering detail: Jesus was eating with unwashed hands. Before the Pharisee was finished pointing out the obvious, Jesus began one of the most uncomfortable dinner moments in history. *"Now you Pharisees cleanse the outside of the cup and of the dish, but inside you are full of greed and wickedness"* (Luke 11:39 ESV). But that was only the beginning. What follows are the words of a vexed and furious Savior. They need no narration or interpretation. Listen:

> *"Woe to you Pharisees, because you give God*
> *a tenth of your mint, rue and all other kinds*

of garden herbs, but you neglect justice and the love of God. You should have practiced the latter without leaving the former undone.

"Woe to you Pharisees, because you love the most important seats in the synagogues and respectful greetings in the marketplaces.

"Woe to you, because you are like unmarked graves, which people walk over without knowing it."

One of the experts in the law answered him, "Teacher, when you say these things, you insult us also."

Jesus replied, "And you experts in the law, woe to you, because you load people down with burdens they can hardly carry, and you yourselves will not lift one finger to help them.

"Woe to you, because you build tombs for the prophets, and it was your ancestors who killed them. So you testify that you approve of what your ancestors did; they killed the prophets, and you build their tombs. Because of this, God in his wisdom said, 'I will send them prophets and apostles, some of whom they will kill and others they will persecute.' Therefore this generation will be held responsible for the blood of all the prophets that has been shed since the beginning of the world, from the blood of Abel to the blood of Zechariah, who was killed between the altar and the sanctuary. Yes, I tell you, this generation will be held responsible for it all.

"Woe to you experts in the law, because you have taken away the key to knowledge. You yourselves have not entered, and you have hindered those who were entering." (Luke 11:42-52 NIV)

Try to imagine what it would be like to be on the other side of these words. How do you defend a furious and pointed indictment from the lips of Jesus? That poor Pharisee had no place to hide that day. He probably never even finished his meal.

What compelled Jesus to go so far as to enter a man's house, sit at his table, and subject him to such verbal repudiation? We can eliminate the idea that Jesus had a grudge; His whole life was love. But He was most certainly picking a fight in an awkward place and time. What does His action say about God's desire for justice? How should this inform our thinking about what God cares about? Jesus' venom was directed at the misappropriation of God's law. The leaders of the people had contorted God's word so much that Jesus could not recognize it. Ignoring justice, they were praising their own virtues, validating their own deeds, erecting their own monuments, burdening the people, and fostering the spread of false righteousness. Jesus saw them as blood-guilty merchants of Satan and malicious hoarders of grace. By their self-indulgence, they managed to turn people away from God for the sake of personal profit.

Since my calling to preach, I have felt the weight and duty to represent God's word with utter care.

When I stand to proclaim from the pulpit, in a classroom, or in casual one-on-one dialogue, I feel as if God is listening to my every word. I try to ensure that in that moment when knowledge passes from my lips and mind to an audience of adults, to a classroom of students, or to an individual that my thoughts are in alignment with God's.

The task of speaking for God is beyond serious; it is terrifying. Yet the Pharisees had forgotten its seriousness and lost the urgent sense that the faith of their listeners was hinged on their every word. The modern church would do well to learn that lesson. However impressive our opinions, they are not worth the words they arrive on. Our duty is to do as Jesus did, to teach as Jesus taught, and to love as Jesus loved, and we should live in dread of the possibility of disappointing God.

The capriciousness of sin's rebellion, the wounds of our families, the impulses that lead to legalism, and the *policing* of God's insatiable grace will keep us in the grip of paralysis. Against all of this, Jesus comes to awaken us, lead us, and defend us. He is our partner in a war we are unable to fight on our own. God is furious when it comes to defending His children. We do not fight alone.

A *"Father of orphans, champion of widows, is God in his holy house. God makes homes for the homeless, leads prisoners to freedom, but leaves rebels to rot in hell"* (Psalm 68:5–6 MSG). Did you catch that? God takes sides. God is on the side of the wounded in battle, the emotionally orphaned, and the religiously scarred. He will fight for our hearts, for we bear His brushstrokes on our hearts. We are marked out for glory. Glory is our destiny. Glory is the shape of our hearts. God made us for this very purpose, to manifest His glory!

8

Something Like Glory

Then Moses said, "Now show me your glory."
~ **Exodus 33:18** NIV

Sometime after my twentieth birthday, I had a recurring dream that I could fly. I flew past mountains and whisked past the tallest trees and buildings. But at the most exciting moment, I would wake up. Most dreams are like that: you always wake up during the good parts. Keep that in mind the next time you dream. But soon after I started college, the dream vanished. I have occasionally wished I could visit that place again and fly to glorious heights, lifted beyond blue skies of wonder. Such was my idea of glory until I read the heart-wrenching cry of Moses: *"Show me Your glory"* (Exodus 33:18 NASB).

THE FACE OF GLORY

Glory comes with every sunrise and glistens in every sunset. It shouts in the thunder and dazzles in the blaze of lightning. In its presence we are amazed; in its absence we destruct. And we all fall short of it by our sinful nature. Glory is the mark, the imprint, the trail that follows God wherever He is.

Its reach is beyond the clouds; the heavens declare it, the earth and all that is in it cannot contain it, and in the temple of God, it fills everything. In the human heart, it is the measure of aliveness. It is the signature of God. Glory is the evidence that God is there. It is a clue to why Moses demanded, *"Show me Your glory."* Let me know that You are there; let me know that it is You. In the next verses, God will reply. Moses will find out that God is dangerous in His glory. It will leave us awestruck and yet set us free. His glory shakes us to the core, yet it leaves us feeling completely alive. Moses took His chances. God, as wise and loving as He is, chose to protect Moses. I will not soon forget the words God spoke to him in these next verses. God in His glory is dangerous:

> And the LORD said, *"I will cause all my good-ness to pass in front of you, and I will proclaim my name, the LORD, in your presence. I will have mercy on whom I will have mercy, and I will have compassion on whom I will have compassion. But,"* he said, *"you cannot see my face, for no one may see me and live."*
>
> Then the LORD said, *"There is a place near me where you may stand on a rock. When my glory passes by, I will put you in a cleft in the rock and cover you with my hand until I have passed by. Then I will remove my hand and you will see*

my back; but my face must not be seen." (Exodus 33:19-23 NIV)

Moses was shielded from God's glory that day. He would not survive such radiance—no one can see God and live. May be that's our cue to avoid being cavalier about God's presence. What Moses longed to see was the full and complete manifestation of God in a face-to-face encounter, in much the same way Adam and Eve encountered Him in the cool of the day. Moses was not allowed to see the face of God, but remember that Adam and Eve did. God came to them fully clothed in His glory—that was the best part of their day. But Satan would rob them of their daily dose of glory. No sunset or sunrise, no mountain or majestic waterfall could measure up to a single moment spent with their Creator. They had God; they had glory. All of humanity has since lived without the measure of glory displayed every day to our first parents. The dream of human existence is the hope to be in God's glorious presence without fear, just as it was in Eden so long ago.

Since that day in Eden when sin turned glory into shame, we humans have been longing for that glory. Moses had seen glimpses, and he wanted to experience it again as Adam and Eve enjoyed it—face to face. In Ezekiel chapter 1, the prophet described what he called *"the likeness of the glory of the LORD"* (Ezekiel 1:28 NIV). This was not the glory of God itself, but its likeness. The manifest glory of God was lost in Eden because face-to-face time with our Creator was no longer possible. Now we see the true nature of sin. It not only robs us of our fellowship, but it also takes away the glory for which we were created—not glory in ourselves but in the Creator Himself. There is something very sinister about sin; it corrupts everything that is glorious. Learning to hate sin amounts to loving fellowship with God and choosing to live in the glory of His presence rather than in shame and squalor.

Glory is not the short-lived bliss celebrated on the pages of magazines or in the empty rants and vulgar lyrics of popular songs. It is not the promise of power, fame, or fortune as in the American Dream. It is not the feeling that you can fly after a night of partying, with the help of alcohol. Glory does not leave you dazed, numb, or hung over. It leaves you alive. Glory is true fulfillment. Darkness flees from it, and sin and death have no power over it. God in His love has made us for this; nothing else has the power to give the sustaining life that only God offers through His glory.

Glory outshines the darkness of our hearts. It helps us to behold God's majesty as we gaze with steadfastness at the one who causes us to glow. The Apostle Paul, who himself encountered God's glory, also reminds us: *"We all, who with unveiled faces contemplate the LORD's glory, are being transformed into his image with ever-increasing glory, which comes from the LORD, who is the Spirit"* (2 Corinthians 3:18 NIV). Glory is not created by earthly conventions or by the imagination of the human spirit; its only source is God. God is like the sun, and we are like the moon. We can only reflect His light; we cannot generate it.

What we seek in ignorance is glory. We have given it other names in our twisted binges of ignorance, but glory alone is our cure. As we give in to its demands, we also contemplate its worth. Contemplation is a noble word. The *American Heritage Dictionary* defines it in this way: "To look at attentively and thoughtfully." And finally, the Greek word is *Meletao* (mel-et-ah´-o,) which means "To take care of, revolve in the mind, or imagine."

Glory shines only in the lives of those who take care of, think on, and give thought to its importance. Remember, we lost the shine in Eden. Glory comes with a cost; it must be contemplated. We behold it only when the mind, heart, and soul turn fully to its discovery. Everything else pales in comparison to the pursuit of it. Glory requires contemplation, and contemplation requires time. Until we are ready to be in God's presence for more than snap prayers and flitting calls in desperate moments of need, we do not know, understand, or deserve such a glorious connection to our Creator. Only those who take it seriously can be worthy of glory.

Glory shines brightest when it rests on the face of God, and Moses wanted to look at God's face. In 2 Corinthians 4:6, Paul expresses Moses' cry: *"For God, who said, 'Let light shine out of darkness,' has shone in our hearts to give the light of the knowledge of the glory of God in the face of Jesus Christ"* (ESV). There it is again. Glory majestically sets on the face of God more than anywhere else in creation. Glory leaves its mark on everything; it refuses to be ignored. Seek it, and you will never be the same again.

The psalmist David understood the need for glory. In Psalm 3:3, he recounted, *"But thou, O LORD, art a shield for me; my glory, and the lifter up of mine head"* (KJV). David experienced pleasure, played with delight, and basked in victory, but he was shielded by glory. It lifted him from distress, elevated him to honor, illuminated his dark caves, and inspired his songs. He could not contemplate life without the glory of God, and neither should we. We must chase after it, whatever the cost. Losing everything in its pursuit is losing nothing, for in finding it, we gain treasure beyond anything of earthly value. No effort must be spared to come face to face with our Maker, lingering long enough to change the shape of our countenance and to lift up our heads. Like a desperate athlete hungry for victory, like a lover seeking the heart of his love, like an adventurer in search of mystery, so must be our search for glory.

Indiana Jones is one of my favorite movie series. In the first installment, *Raiders of the Lost Ark*, famed archaeologist/adventurer Dr. Henry "Indiana" Jones (played by Harrison Ford) is sent on a mission by the U.S. government to locate the Ark of the Covenant. Insatiable and daring in his search, he leaves no stones unturned and no webs unbroken, for he must find this Ark. Nothing will stop him. If you've seen the movie, you know how many times he came close to losing his life on his thrilling recovery missions. It was an adventure from which the threat of death did not hinder him.

Why was it so desirable to Indiana Jones? Was it his love of archeology, the thrill of danger, or something more? Could it be glory? The old archeologist may have wanted to catch a glimpse of glory, but why, and what was it? Many have tried to reach for glory, yet they have failed to unveil the breadth and reach of it. Even so, I join this chorus of wise men to make my feeble attempt at understanding this idea that is so riveting and meaningful. Upon more reflection, I now know that my recurring dream of flying fell infinitely short of true glory. The immense pleasure derived from my dream was not in the dream itself but in what it produced. In other words, I enjoyed this dream not because I was dreaming, but because I was delighted by a measure of grandness that propelled me past my own limited spaces.

I am now struck by the clarity of God's parables. All of our dreams of grandeur—wonder, fame, power, or pleasure—are but human attempts to grasp His indescribable glory. In moments like these, we may wish we could return all wasted moments, all unworthiness, and all vile thoughts and actions in exchange for the only indestructible good—the glory of God. All who seek Him with ruthless fervor stand to gain everything and lose nothing.

A CONSUMING FIRE

Moses was one such person. His experience, described in Exodus chapter 19, demonstrates why God is both approachable and dangerous. God had just ordered Moses up Mount Sinai, where He would give him the Ten Commandments. Three months later, Moses reached the top of the mountain on Shavuot, the Feast of Harvest. This is now the Feast of Pentecost, which takes place on the fiftieth day after Passover as described in the New Testament. Moses and all the companies of Israel were about to encounter the seriousness of glory:

> *On the morning of the third day there was thunder and lightning, with a thick cloud over the mountain, and a very loud trumpet blast. Everyone in the camp trembled. Then Moses led the people out of the camp to meet with God, and they stood at the foot of the mountain. Mount Sinai was covered with smoke, because the LORD descended on it in fire. The smoke billowed up from it like smoke from a furnace, and the whole mountain trembled violently. As the sound of the trumpet grew louder and louder, Moses spoke and the voice of God answered him.*
>
> *The LORD descended to the top of Mount Sinai and called Moses to the top of the mountain. So Moses went up and the LORD said to him, "Go down and warn the people so they do not force their way through to see the LORD and many of*

them perish. Even the priests, who approach the
Lord, must consecrate themselves, or the Lord
will break out against them."

Moses said to the Lord, "The people cannot
come up Mount Sinai, because you yourself
warned us, 'Put limits around the mountain and
set it apart as holy.'"

The Lord replied, "Go down and bring Aaron
up with you. But the priests and the people must
not force their way through to come up to the
Lord, or he will break out against them." (Exodus
19:16–24 niv)

Glory is a serious thing! The same loving God who
met Moses in a burning bush and allowed him to see
a glimpse of His face now warns with fierce threatening: "Don't come near." God is serious about His
glory. He will share it with no man and will defend it
with intensity. *"Our God is a consuming fire"* (Hebrews
12:29 niv).

It's easy for us to sit in our creature comfort and
talk about God, casually and without fear. However,
this passage from Exodus must enlighten our understanding. This picture of glory is anything but comfortable. The people were told twice to not come near. God
descended and Moses had to stand still in his place. It
is as if God were saying, "Take me for granted at your
own risk."

The people were told to consecrate themselves,
wash their clothing, and abstain from sexual activity.

Why were they told to do these things? God, in His glory, requires holiness. He approaches us on His terms. This should shape our relationship with God, for the inapproachable has now been made approachable in Christ. God is God and we are not. God is holy, and we need to work out our salvation with fear and trembling. Why were the Israelites told to have this fear, but to remember the limits of their humanity in the midst of glory? It's because glory is no small thing.

When we lose the fear of God's glory, we fall prey to sin. This loss of fear is what drove Adam and Eve from paradise. When they lost the sacred mystery of His glory, they fumbled in their thinking. Instead of seeking His glory, they sought their own. Satan's lie, that they would be as wise as God, did the trick. Moses understood the danger of taking God's presence for granted—he would not take one step without staying in God's presence. In Exodus 35:15, Moses refused to proceed unless God was with Israel. We would also do well to proceed only when God in His glory is leading.

EXPOSED BY GLORY

Who can forget the words God spoke to Adam after He created him? *"But of the tree of the knowledge of good and evil you shall not eat, for in the day that you eat of it you shall surely die"* (Genesis 2:17 ESV). Since that day in Eden, we have never escaped the horrible consequence of sin. Sin is a virus in the garden of the heart; all that comes into its path will die. But there is an antidote. There is but one remedy effective against the viciousness of sin—it is called *glory*.

Isaiah the prophet was exposed by this glory, and he was never the same. His response was surprising, counter to what was expected for a righteous man. Listen to his words:

> *In the year that King Uzziah died, I saw the LORD, high and exalted, seated on a throne; and the train of his robe filled the temple. Above him were seraphim, each with six wings: With two wings they covered their faces, with two they covered their feet, and with two they were flying. And they were calling to one another:*
>
> *"Holy, holy, holy is the LORD Almighty; the whole earth is full of his glory."*
>
> *At the sound of their voices the doorposts and thresholds shook and the temple was filled with smoke.*
>
> *"Woe to me!" I cried. "I am ruined! For I am a man of unclean lips, and I live among a people of unclean lips, and my eyes have seen the King, the LORD Almighty."*
>
> *Then one of the seraphim flew to me with a live coal in his hand, which he had taken with tongs from the altar. With it he touched my mouth and said, "See, this has touched your lips; your*

guilt is taken away and your sin atoned for."
(Isaiah 6:1–7 NIV*)*

Here, Isaiah disclosed the time and season of his great unraveling. This encounter with the glorious God in the form of a vision occurred in the year of King Uzziah's death. What he saw, felt, and heard left him deeply and irrevocably changed. Uzziah (also known as Azariah) was king over Judah from around 809 to 757 BC. Chosen by the people at the age of sixteen after the death of his father Ahaziah, this young king reigned for fifty-two years over Judah and led them to their greatest prosperity since the reign of Solomon. His devotion to God's worship remained intact until he became enamored with his success and attempted to burn incense on the altar (typically done by the priest) and was suddenly smitten with leprosy. Uzziah died (2 Chronicles 26:23) and was buried with his fathers, leaving a deep sense of uncertainty in Judah.

It was during this season of national and spiritual insecurity that Isaiah saw the glory of God in the temple. Isaiah was reminded that the true King of Judah was alive and well, sitting on His throne, and gloriously ruling. His throne, unlike that of the deceased king, was as indestructible as His glory. Then Isaiah saw a host of heavenly beings worshiping the living God. They were calling in magnificent antiphony: *"Holy, holy, holy is the* LORD *Almighty; the whole earth is full of His glory"* (Isaiah 6:3 NIV).

The sounds of their voices shook the foundations, and the door posts of the temple began to shake violently. Then Isaiah saw that the temple was filling with smoke. This smoke symbolized the presence of God, which left no empty space. In this, God's grandness was revealed. Isaiah cried, "Woe is me." He had just seen the Lord, the glorious one. The prophet had suddenly lost his footing.

Here was a righteous man, a prophet of God, and yet his immediate response was humble recognition of his unworthiness before God. That is what glory does; it puts us in our place. God's response to Isaiah is both refining and life giving. Just as Isaiah beholds his unworthiness, *one of the seraphim flew to him with a coal in his hand, which was taken from the altar* (Isaiah 6:6). With one touch, his sins were washed away, as if they had never been. He had been exposed; and yet he was set free.

One would expect a burning coal to cause pain and inflict damage, but in this case, it represented a burning fire of Isaiah's purification and a restoration, enabling him to remain in the glorious presence of God. This restoration caused Isaiah to utter the next words of surrender to God's plan of salvation: "Here am I! Send me." Humbled by what he had witnessed, Isaiah volunteered to go, just as we all should volunteer to be ambassadors and witnesses of God's glory.

GLORY REFLECTED

Stephen arrived on the Jewish scene without fanfare, entourage, or great recognition. But before long, his deeds and life captured the attention of everyone in Israel. He was, for all practical purposes, an apostle without a portfolio. Yet Scripture described him as a man who was *"full of the Spirit and of wisdom,"* according to Acts 6:3 (NASB). Further, we are told in Acts 6:5 that he was *"full of faith and of the Holy Spirit."* By the power of the Spirit who led him, Stephen performed many signs and wonders, stunning his critics and bringing fear to those in Israel who were paying attention. These wonders would also cost him.

As a result of those mighty deeds, some began to oppose him with great zeal and fury. They accused him of speaking blasphemy against Moses and the law, which forced him to defend himself in the longest sermon in the book of Acts. The curious crowd looked intently as his face became like that of an angel before the Sanhedrin council. Then he began to chronicle the lives of Abraham and Moses, Israel's trials in Egypt, God's deliverance through the Red Sea, the rejection of God's law, and the worship of a golden calf at Mount Sinai. He reminded them of Israel's rejection of the prophets, calling them a stiffed-necked people. With that, they were stirred with great anger toward Stephen:

> *When the members of the Sanhedrin heard this, they were furious and gnashed their teeth at*

him. But Stephen, full of the Holy Spirit, looked up to heaven and saw the glory of God, and Jesus standing at the right hand of God. "Look," he said, "I see heaven open and the Son of Man standing at the right hand of God."

At this they covered their ears and, yelling at the top of their voices, they all rushed at him, dragged him out of the city and began to stone him. Meanwhile, the witnesses laid their coats at the feet of a young man named Saul.

While they were stoning him, Stephen prayed, "Lord Jesus, receive my spirit." Then he fell on his knees and cried out, "Lord, do not hold this sin against them." When he had said this, he fell asleep. (Acts 7:54–60 NIV)

The man who lived in the power of the Holy Spirit and wisdom now faced the wrath of his enemies. But armed only with the presence of God, he stood his ground against their fury. They would take his life that day but not his witness; his voice still echoes across the years. Why is it that this man could raise his voice in praise even as his earthly existence was pouring out onto a Jerusalem pavement? What made him so radiant that even his persecutors had to look away from the glow on his face? How was he able to see the glory of Christ in heaven while still standing on earth? The answers to these questions define what glory is. It is the presence of God, reflected.

Glory is part of God's redemptive character. His desire is that we reflect it by calling sinners to behold the glorious God of our redemption. Moses would do anything just to catch a glimpse of it, and when he did, others saw on his face the mark of God's presence. Isaiah encountered it and was humbled as he beheld his Maker in heaven, with angels at His service and His glory filling all heaven and earth. He also went on to tell others. Stephen lived for God's glory by the power of the Spirit, speaking about God through signs and wonders. He was not afraid of death, for God's glory, which he sought in living, was his defense in dying. He needed no proof or explanation because he saw the face of God.

We cannot escape the primacy of God's glory in everything present and absent, earthly and eternal, visible and invisible, secular and sacred, living and dead. God fills everything, everywhere, in every time and season, both now and forevermore. But with the coming of Jesus to earth, God's glory was most clearly manifested. This was no myth; God Himself stepped out from behind the curtains of eternity onto the stage of human existence. He outshined the sun itself in His glory.

9

Before Sunrise

As a child I received instruction both in the Bible and in the Talmud. I am a Jew, but I am enthralled by the luminous figure of the Nazarene. ... No one can read the Gospels without feeling the actual presence of Jesus. His personality pulsates in every word. No myth is filled with such life.
~ Albert Einstein

O n a festive day in Cana of Galilee, Jesus arrived with His disciples for the event of their week, a wedding. His mother also came. We don't know the names of the bride and groom or the servants Jesus spoke to. What we do know is that in this very common earthly event, Jesus revealed His glory: *"This beginning of His signs Jesus did in Cana of Galilee, and manifested His glory, and His disciples believed in Him"* (John 2:11 NASB). When the wine ran out, Jesus' mother approached Him, saying, "They have no wine." Despite His earlier objection and a slight rebuke, He commanded that six empty stone jars (each one weighing about thirty gallons) be filled with water. After filling them, the water miraculously turned into wine of the finest quality. Jesus had performed His first public sign!

To everyone's astonishment, Jesus had just done what was beyond human ability. The man born in Bethlehem and raised in Nazareth had disclosed His true identity. This son of a carpenter was really the Son of God, this was the Messiah, the Promised One. The glory of all the ages had appeared among men, and they beheld Him with unfettered eyes.

The Creator Himself was among the created, and only now did they know it. *"The Word became flesh and made his dwelling among us. We have seen his glory, the glory of the one and only Son, who came from the Father, full of grace and truth"* (John 1:14 NIV).

This truly was the Son of God, the promised seed of the woman who would bruise the serpent's head. Three short years after His miracle in Cana, Jesus would face His ancient foe. The Serpent of Eden would meet the Lion of Judah. Satan, the sower of havoc, would be on the receiving end this time; his defeat would be decisive.

THE PROMISE

When Satan trespassed the Garden of Eden, he did more than deceive Adam and Eve; he came between two people in love. How curious that Jesus began His earthly ministry bringing joy to two people in love. Eden represented the happiest time for humanity, when love between a man, his wife, and his God was blissful, simple, and satisfying. But sin's poison spilled into everything in paradise, leaving Adam and Eve in isolation from God and themselves. Satan won a battle that day, but the war was hardly over.

Round two would result in a much different outcome. Centuries after Eden, Jesus returned to win the war that would redraw the landscape of history. He came, as advertised, to *crush the head of Satan* and restore paradise. Satan's lie threatened to cripple the first marriage and the future of their offspring with his wine of deceit, the fruit that brought death. Jesus, the embodiment of truth, began His earthly ministry with wine that celebrated life: *"The thief comes only to steal and kill and destroy; I have come that they may have life, and have it to the full"* (John 10:10 NIV).

More than any other passage in Scripture, Genesis 3:15 communicates the triumph of the seed of the woman: *"And I will put enmity between you and the woman, and between your offspring and hers; he will crush your head, and you will strike his heel"* (NIV). Enmity is a fighting word. It means hostility or extreme hatred. Hostility would define human history, but in the end, there would be a victor.

This enmity between Satan and the woman is the first evidence that the two were natural enemies. Satan succeeded in coaxing Eve into believing that he was a partner in a curious adventure of forbidden ambitions. Eve had opened her eyes to the true nature of her relationship with the serpent, recognizing that his hostile intention was to destroy her and her offspring. She would no longer converse with the stranger in the garden as he was no longer welcome, yet she could not get rid of him. Sin had spread like a virus.

Everyone feels the effects of sin's venom, plunged deep into our veins. It would have killed our souls if not for Jesus. We would be laid waste in a pile of death at the feet of the ancient serpent. *"Were not the right man on our side, the man of God's own choosing."*[16] This alone should weigh upon our conscience before we choose to listen to the deceitful voice of our enemy. We must be awakened to the same realization that Eve experienced: the serpent is not our friend. He urges us to take the forbidden fruit; his purpose is our harm.

Jesus came as promised to crush Satan and retake the paradise taken from Adam and Eve. He came to our defense in a city where death and terror reigned and where tragedies of all kinds never cease. We've been chained, hands and hearts, to habits that enslave us. The law of God could set us free, but we disregard it. We wake up every day a lost and broken people at war within ourselves. Prejudice still haunts our history, and though death still threatens, the bells of Easter are ringing in the distance.

In the year 1800, the French Emperor Napoleon invaded Austria, and they came to a town called Feldkirk. It was not defended, and it looked as if there would be no resistance. On the Saturday night before Easter, Napoleon's troops were approximately six miles from Feldkirk. The Christians in that town gathered in their churches and prayed all night for deliverance from

Napoleon's army. All through that night, Napoleon marched his army toward the town.

> On Easter Sunday morning, when the sun came up, the bells of all the churches in the town pealed out their song of victory, the resurrection of Jesus Christ. Because Napoleon had introduced a new calendar with a ten-day cycle instead of seven, he had no Christian calendar reference. Napoleon and his troops didn't know it was Easter Sunday morning. They thought the bells were signaling jubilation because the Austrian army had come into the city and the people were rejoicing that they would be defended. On that assumption, Napoleon chose to retreat. Those Easter bells and the message they rang out meant that there would be peace in that countryside. There never was a French-Austrian battle for the town of Feldkirk.[17]

Jesus' death and resurrection would signal the retreat of Satan's marching army of death. The merchants of death would soon meet the Lord of life. They would quiver in surrender. Bodies laid waste in death would open their eyes, reentering life. Fathers and sisters who had already said their goodbyes welcomed back their loved ones, in a preview of coming attractions. The words of Paul were gaining traction and would soon shake the echo chambers of hell: *"Death has been swallowed up in victory"* (1 Corinthians 15:54 NIV).

FRANTIC FEARS

Jesus' travels took him from one beleaguered city and town to another, preaching about the kingdom of God. Since His first miracle in Cana of Galilee, He caused the world around Him to wrestle with the possibility that He was more than the son of a carpenter. Jesus fended off Satan, compelled the obedience of His followers, delivered the most famous sermon in history, calmed the storm, and healed all kinds of sickness and disease. But now we see Jesus as the life-giver, even as we are introduced to a grieving ruler in Matthew 9:18–26, where Jesus' conversation on fasting was abruptly interrupted at the news of a girl's death.

While He was in the midst of teaching, a synagogue ruler came and knelt before Him, saying, "My daughter has just died, but come and lay Your hand on her, and she will live." Jesus, feeling compassion, began to follow him home, but a woman who had suffered twelve years from a discharge came up behind Jesus and touched Him. She believed that touching even the *fringe* of His garment would make her well. Jesus declared her in good health; she was in that moment healed. Then He then entered the ruler's house to the tune of a flute, signifying death and mourning.

Imagine what the ruler's wife and other children were thinking as they pondered the unrealized dreams and wishes of the little girl. In the midst of their questions and anguish, Jesus entered the room, not to mourn, but to inaugurate a new era in the conflict between life and death. He quickly dismissed them, saying, *"Go away, for the girl is not dead but sleeping"* (Matthew 9:24 ESV). Sleeping? They began to laugh at Him. Then Jesus did the unthinkable: He took the dead girl by the hand, and in one swoop, brought her back to life.

I stood in the morgue alongside my sister in 2008 and looked in disbelief at the horrific face of death. I had traveled twelve hours by air to my home country on the news of my mom's passing. There I was, tired, broken, diminished, and at a loss for reason. This was Tuesday, June 17, 2008. The Thursday before, I had talked with my mom and prayed with her over the phone; I was confident she would be okay. Five days later, I was standing there feeling as if my body, mind, and soul were squeezed together to the point of bursting. This was not how things were supposed to go. This was not what I prayed for, but I had no power over death. It was final. My mom was gone. Out of nowhere, the raging rush of death had swept her away with its currents, and I could do nothing.

How much I wished I could pray her back to life; indeed, I prayed with overflowing tears, "Jesus, please come to my rescue." Memories were rushing in like the waters that washed her away. My heart was beating like a drum without sequence or rhythm, and anger soon took over. Death had stolen my guardian angel, my first love, my mother. Refusing my sister's consoling, I pleaded with even heavier tears, "Why?" As my tears subsided, the words of Paul began to reset the clock of my heart: *"If in this life only we have hope in Christ, we are of all men the most pitiable"* (1 Corinthians 15:19 NKJV). I stopped to consider Paul's words. Then I heard the calming voice of Jesus say, *"Let not your heart be troubled; you believe in God, believe also in Me"* (John 14:1 NKJV). I still believe.

For all who have experienced the pain of death, in any age, the despair of finality is felt by those left behind. But the coming of Jesus in the flesh gives new hope: *"But come and put your hand on her, and she will live"* (Matthew 9:18 NIV). Against all hope, against all reason, this father believed Jesus had the power of life and power over death. No one else in all of history can stake that claim.

In the gospels of Mark, Luke, and John, Jairus is identified as the father of the young girl. He was a ruler in his local synagogue, which was an important position in those days. Jairus came to Jesus in an unlikely fashion for a man of his stature. He fell at the feet of Jesus, an act of both faith and desperation. He believed that Jesus was his only option, and faith was his vehicle. Remarkably, the name Jairus means "He will awaken," which was a possible sign that more than his daughter's life was at stake. Watching Jesus raise his little girl to life must have ignited in him a new awakening of who Jesus was.

Nothing is as compelling as watching the dead come back to life. That fact alone separates Christianity from other religions. Jesus' followers and skeptics alike had witnessed the grandness of His healings, signs, and wonders of every kind, including walking on water. Raising the dead would catapult His ministry into the stratosphere. His other miracles may have been stunning, but no one had ever seen the dead raised to life. He said to her, "Talitha, arise" (Mark 5:41). The news of this miracle spread like wildfire.

We can't be sure why Jesus chose that particular moment to manifest His glory, but we can be certain of its impact. We can also be certain of His motivation. *"Since the children have flesh and blood, he too shared in their humanity so that by his death he might break the power of him who holds the power of death— that is, the devil—and free those who all their lives were held in slavery by their fear of death"* (Hebrew 2:14–15 NIV). Ground that had swallowed life into darkness was forced to give it back that day. A ruler received his daughter, and the prison of death cracked wide open. The sun had risen, and a new day had dawned.

WEEPING SISTERS

Two friends of Jesus had lost their brother, Lazarus of Bethany, to the frightening sting of death. Lazarus was himself a friend of Jesus. One of his sisters, Mary, first met Jesus with adoring worship, anointing His feet and wiping them dry with her hair. Jesus had earlier received the report of Lazarus' illness, but He remained where He was for two more days.

Jesus had already told His disciples that Lazarus' illness would not lead to death (John 11:4) but would be for the glory of God. Stunned as they often were, his disciples were surprised when Jesus announced that Lazarus had, in His words, *fallen asleep*. Puzzled, they said, "If he has fallen asleep, he will recover" (v. 12). But by that time, Lazarus was already dead.

Jesus, along with His disciples, headed to Bethany where all would see *the glory of God*. By the time Jesus got there, Lazarus had been dead for four full days. "Lord, if you had been here, my brother would not have died," Mary wept with bitter tears.

Moved by Mary's tears, "Jesus wept" (John 11:35). How amazing that this face of the very glory of God wept tears of sadness for a friend. After He had prayed to His Father, Jesus called out to Lazarus in a loud voice: "Come out!" Immediately, the dead man walked out of the grave. Still wrapped in cloth around his face and body, Jesus commanded them to "unbind him and to let him go" (John 11:44). After four days in death's cold valley, Lazarus returned to life. There could be no mistake about this glory revealed; it was life-giving and powerful. Jesus again demonstrated that He had power over death.

Unlike the case of Jairus' daughter, who was dead only for a short while, Lazarus had been dead for days. One might find some theory for why a recently dead person could be made alive, but who can explain a decaying body's chances at life? We have become accustomed to rationalizing everything and anything that we can't explain. We are a cynical generation. But raising a dead man after four days leaves room for no cynics. These resurrections were down payments on God's promise to crush Satan for his breach of paradise.

Hints of this promise can be found in the words of Jesus Himself to a grieving Martha at the tomb of her brother: *"Did I not tell you that if you believed you would see the glory of God?"* (John 11:40 esv). Death no longer posed a threat. All who put their trust in Jesus are inoculated against the venom of death. Its sting has no power; its scare has no danger. All those who lived in slavery to the fear of death had the antidote. The valley of the shadow of death was only a shadow, driven away by the light of the Son of God.

But as news of Lazarus' resurrection began to spread throughout the region, an angry mob of chief priests and Pharisees sought to silence Jesus. Afraid that the nation would turn to Him, they plotted to kill Jesus. Cynicism is not only the disease of the religiously ignorant; it is also the cancer of religious tyrants. The very people who were to prepare the way for Jesus' coming were scrambling to defeat His mission. Their brand of religion suffocated life. In the end, they would try to kill Lazarus, fearing he would remind them of Jesus' imposing presence.

DAYBREAK

The sky was overcast; a dark cloud hung over Jerusalem. A strong east wind raised a dusty gale. Whispers and airy stillness pervaded the city, now shaken by the death of Jesus. The natural order was disturbed as all heaven and earth cried out. There were signs in the heavens and stirrings in the hearts of men and women. The centurion's declaration, *"Truly this man was the Son of God"* (Mark 15:39 ESV), echoed throughout the city's alleys and dusty paths. From the king's palace to the hushed voices of women gathering water, the event of Black Friday was being weighed on a scale that set hope against despair.

Still shaking from the jolt of bereavement, Jesus' disciples hunkered down in fearful silence. It had been three days since their Lord was beaten, mocked, crucified, dead, and buried. The same crowds that cheered for Him in Jerusalem demanded that a murderer be freed and that Jesus be crucified. Barabbas, a vile soul and a taker of life, guilty of his crime, went free that day. The Sinless One, the Giver of Life, was betrayed by violent men. Even his friends denied him as He walked down a dusty road; they watched, but from afar. "He never told us this would happen," they insisted in their confusion and grief. Were they not listening?

The Son of Man came to earth on a mission—death was his destiny and life our gain. *"And he began to teach them that the Son of Man must suffer many things and be rejected by the elders and the chief priests and the scribes and be killed, and after three days rise again. And he said this plainly. And Peter took him aside and began to rebuke him. But turning and seeing his disciples, he rebuked Peter and said, 'Get behind me, Satan! For you are not setting your mind on the things of God, but on the things of man.'"* (Mark 8:31–33 ESV). Jesus knew that His path would be difficult, but He endured it with courage, looking always to His Father in whom He trusted for vindication.

Even the most dedicated of Jesus' followers could not grasp—or did not want to grasp—the unimaginable suffering of the Messiah. The following was written long ago: *"For you will not abandon my soul to Sheol, or let your holy one see corruption"* (Psalm 16:10 ESV). Jesus knew His death and resurrection had been predicted.

Three times in Mark's gospel alone, Jesus told His disciples that he would die and then rise again on the third day. Please examine these instances and see for yourself. First, in Mark 8:31: *"He began to teach them that the Son of Man must suffer many things and be rejected by the elders and the chief priests and the scribes and be killed, and after three days rise again"* (ESV). Second, He plainly told them in Mark 9:31, *"The Son of Man is going to be delivered into the hands of men, and they will kill him. And when he is killed, after three days he will rise"* (ESV). Finally, in Mark 10:33–34, Jesus loudly proclaimed it to them, saying, *"See, we are going up to Jerusalem, and the Son of Man will be delivered over to the chief priests and the scribes, and they will condemn him to death and deliver him over to the Gentiles. And they will mock him and spit on him, and flog him and kill him. And after three days he will rise"* (ESV).

But the disciples were surprised and stunned by what had happened. Let us not be so harsh and rebuke their ignorance, since we are guilty of the same crime. We are creatures who hear what we want to hear, much like Peter who, in his self-loathing, advocated a very human desire—what we love must remain with us at all times. Peter could not afford to lose Jesus because Jesus was good for Peter. So it is with us: we refuse to let go of anything we are attached to. But behind their wall of anguish was the sense that they had not seen or heard the last of Jesus.

Luke paints a colorful picture of the questions raised three days after Jesus' death. He does so by narrating a conversation between two of Jesus' disciples who were traveling to the town of Emmaus. The account is found in Luke 24:13–35. He begins, *"Now that same day two of them were going to a village called Emmaus, about seven miles from Jerusalem. They were talking with each other about everything that had happened. As they talked and discussed these things with each other, Jesus himself came up and walked along with them; but they were kept from recognizing him"* (vv. 13–16 NIV).

Still unaware of the stranger's identity, Jesus asked them, *"What are you discussing together as you walk along?"* (v. 17). This is certainly a typical way to introduce oneself into a conversation: "What are you talking about?" However, there is more than meets the eye. The word translated as *discussing* means "to argue about." What were they arguing about? At Jesus' question, the two travelers *"stood still, their faces downcast"* (v. 17). One of them, named Cleopas, asked him, *"Are you the only one visiting Jerusalem who does not know the things that have happened there in these days?"* (v. 18).

Then unfolded the news of what had happened three days before in Jerusalem. The discussion involved two men struggling between doubt and rising hope. On one hand, they wrestled with the idea that Jesus, who had raised the dead, was Himself swept into its darkness; while on the other hand, they held on to their faith that this moment, which seemed to be the end, was a strange new beginning.

In the meantime, Mary Magdalene and two other women had risen early, while it was still dark, and had gone to the tomb of Jesus. What they saw and heard sent them racing back to tell Peter and John. *"Two men stood by them in dazzling apparel. And as they were frightened and bowed their faces to the ground, the men said to them, 'Why do you seek the living among the dead? He is not here, but has risen'"* (Luke 24:4–6 ESV). John chapter 20 records that Peter and John raced to the tomb when they heard the news. John arrived first, stopping at the entrance to peer inside. But Peter, the ever-impetuous one, ran straight into the empty tomb, and John followed suit. Only then did they understand what Jesus meant when He promised to rise again from the dead. (See John 20:3–10.) Imagine what they were thinking.

As they returned to their homes, Peter and John must have replayed scenes of Jesus' betrayal by Judas, His arrest by the high priests, and the drowning darkness that had overcome them. They remembered Jesus being blindfolded, mocked, and beaten by men of unclean hands—hands that shed innocent blood.

"Prophesy! Who is it that struck you?" was their insult (Luke 22:64 ESV). They also recalled the injustice He suffered in the subverted courts of Herod and Pilate.

Peter remembered how Simon of Cyrene assisted Jesus by carrying His cross up the hill. Peter wondered why he did not suffer with Him and carry the cross himself. He had denied Jesus with vulgar defiance. Oh, how he wished to take it all back. Then finally, Peter and John replayed scenes of Jesus' hands and feet nailed to the cross, as His body jolted with horrifying agony. His cry, *"It is finished!"* tormented them with guilt and piecing regret. Mary interrupted their troubled silence. *"I have seen the Lord,"* she said (John 20:18 ESV). Their hearts began to turn, stirring with the joy of a new day. This was not any new day—it was the best day of their lives. Questions were answered, doubts were settled, life was reborn, and hope was rising.

Boldness came over Peter and John, causing them to become like invincible men ready to do battle. Joy overtook them like a river, washing away their fears and regrets. The serpent's weapon of death was broken so it was no longer a threat to the children of God. The transaction of redemption was paid in full with nothing owed. Paradise was restored, never again to be lost. The era of darkness met its end in the blazing daybreak of God. An army of the dead rose to life, filling the streets in celebration and hailing the King of Life. Everyone was now unafraid of the serpent since he was crushed by the seed of the woman, as promised so long ago. Mankind was free.

It had been less than seven days since Jesus had stared death in the face and beaten back its deadly plot. Now His disciples stood tall as men of courage, bold and audacious, raising their battle cry. They stood on recaptured ground. The battle lines were indeed redrawn, and the disciples took a huge step forward in their march for freedom. They had no fear; they had just seen their Lord walk out of the grave. Nothing, including death, threatened them.

You and I were made for that kind of freedom. Bondage was never meant for us, but since the beginning, we've been trapped in the grip of everything from fleeting pleasure to an alluring dance with death. What Jesus did on that Jerusalem day released us from both the fear of living and the fear of dying. The word for that is *freedom*.

Freedom is the free reign of life. If we understand this correctly, we see why it would take the death of God's Son to bring it about. Franklin D. Roosevelt said of freedom: "In the truest sense, freedom cannot be bestowed; it must be achieved." He was right. It is for this reason that Jesus' death was not merely a moral example to inspire us. Instead, His death—indeed, His whole life—displayed how the infinite love of God achieved our freedom. The only fitting response to this is loyalty, which makes us followers of Christ. His life, death, and resurrection enlist us in that new reign of life that we were first promised in Eden.

Adam and Eve were the first to be enlisted in this epic adventure. They loved their freedom and wanted just a little bit more of it. Their freedom could have been maintained through obedience, and yet they followed a downward spiral that we know all too well.

Jesus' first disciples experienced His freedom first-hand. As they followed Him out of Bethany, they knew and felt an aliveness that can only be described as raw gumption. But Jesus blessed them and departed into heaven from where He promised to come again to receive them.

They blinked and without notice, Jesus lifted up into the clouds and into the glory of God. He was carried into heaven, but He left them with a promise. The same two men who appeared to them in white robes with the news that "He had risen" now greeted them: *"'Men of Galilee,' they said, 'why do you stand here looking into the sky? This same Jesus, who has been taken from you into heaven, will come back in the same way you have seen him go into heaven'"* (Acts 1:11 NIV).

Like you, my eyes have wept bitter tears. Life has brought us all to the verge of breaking. But tears are more than a language; they are a road map to a place where all things broken become new. If we allow it, our brokenness will lead us to that place of healing, joy, peace, and faith that reveals that nothing is ever lost. God counts our tears and dries them in His love. Jairus felt that comfort in seeing his daughter come back to life. Mary and Martha saw their brother alive after he was four days in the grave. Jesus' disciples waited in anguish but saw their Lord again. Jesus ascended to sit on the throne of heaven, where He rules at God's mighty right hand of power.

As I imagine this picture of Jesus at God's right hand, I find great comfort in knowing that my mother is alive with Jesus today, because He reigns over death. It is true that death is a paper tiger. I could not bring my mother back to life again. You can't either. Yet we believe they are more alive in heaven than we are on earth. They have seen the face of glory with unfettered eyes. They live in the presence of Jesus daily. They have the answers to the questions we're asking. Because of Jesus, mourning, tearful, frantic, and weeping children are not afraid anymore. We have seen the worst, and it has not broken us. We are stronger, better, wiser, and more vigilant, and we are ready to join the Lion of Judah in His triumphant roar over the Serpent of Paradise and all his cohorts. Together we will enter God's new garden with Jesus and experience the richness God always intended for us. That's where everything will be radically, eternally changed. That's what we are waiting for. Heaven is our hope.

10

Things of Earth, Dreams of Heaven

Heaven wheels above you, displaying to you her eternal glories, and still your eyes are on the ground.
~ Dante Alighieri

Things break on impact when they fall against the stubborn law of gravity. In my childhood home was a china cabinet. It was often under lock and key, and I often wondered why. One day, to my great delight, I unexpectedly found the cabinet open. I walked right up to it, poking my hand through to the hidden treasures inside. There was a variety of cups, jars, glasses, plates, and vases. Some were engraved with flower gardens, nature scenes, or ancient cities. I was drawn to a golden vase about nine inches high that dazzled in the sunlight. It was teasing my eyes.

I reached into the cabinet to grab it in a single motion. Then I heard a sound. Turning in fear, I dropped the vase. The next second, I was looking at a spread of broken pieces scattered throughout the living room as my mom walked in. The damage was done. Nothing could put the pieces back together. My curiosity turned a golden treasure into a wasted pile of broken glass, never again to be assembled. My disobedience had a cost, and as I remember, it hurt.

It's hard to miss the similarity between my story of a broken vase and what happened in Eden, where the golden vase of human innocence was broken. Adam and Eve, tempted by intrigue and curiosity, could not resist the impulse to discover what was hidden in God's mysterious cabinet reserved for His free creatures. Millennia after, we are still searching for the broken pieces first shattered in the ancient garden. Every generation struggles with the same question: How can we mend this brokenness? We all know that we are not what we were meant to be; we're broken. Will we find what's missing? Where do we look for it?

FLAMING SWORDS

Eden was Adam and Eve's home, and the Tree of Life was their shelter. But they were no longer welcomed in Eden. East of the garden, where they once had fellowship with their Creator, stood an army of angels as well as a flaming sword guarding the Tree of Life. And it was for their good. Their threat level had risen, and God had to intervene before greater danger befell them. Adam and Eve had lost the right to be in God's presence. They had to go. How dare God deprive them? Did He not make them free?

"So He drove the man out; and at the east of the garden of Eden He stationed the cherubim and the

flaming sword which turned every direction to guard the way to the tree of life" (Genesis 3:24 NASB). Two things stand out in this verse. First, we meet the *cherubim,* creatures who protect the holiness of God. They would appear over the mercy seat, where God would meet man once a year on the Day of Atonement. These cherubim (plural) stood guard at the east of Eden with a flaming sword (singular) to guard the entrance to the Tree of Life. The presence of these creatures highlights the cosmic shift in the relationship between man and his Creator. Adam and Eve had free access, but now threatening cherubim created a wall between God and the apple of His eyes. That's what sin does.

Second, we notice the flaming sword. Swords are weapons of war. The Old Testament mentions the word over four hundred times, depicting both physical and spiritual warfare. God and man have been at war since man's first disobedience. In this war, however, the victory is not for God but for us. He hurts over the sin that separates us—not for what He stands to lose but for what we stand to lose. He was pleading with Adam, as He pleads with us, to repent and re-enter His presence. "God revealed this to Adam, not to drive him to despair, but to oblige and quicken him to look for life and happiness in the promised seed, by whom the flaming sword is removed."[18]

God knew all too well how man was capable of trickery. Having missed the mark (Romans 3:23), we too must pass through the flaming sword, which is the Word of God: *"For the word of God is living and active, sharper than any two-edged sword"* (Hebrews 4:12 ESV). The Word of God cuts both ways. It defends the presence and holiness of God and proves us by its fire. Scripture also mentions the sword of the Spirit (Ephesians 6:17), which is the Word of God. We can't approach God willy-nilly or through clever arguments, payoffs, or name-dropping. We must come through the flaming sword, God's Word.

We live in an age of easy access, easy love, and easy grace. Things are owed to us simply because we want them. Wishing and having are often not very far apart in our age of entitlements and rights. Much of what we want can be ordered with ease, by flicking a finger or punching a button. Yet the things we need the most take time, require sacrifice, and command attention, none of which we seem willing to do. Adam, like all of us, more than likely wanted to re-enter God's presence, in spite of his disobedience.

God's presence is for those who obey, which neither Adam nor any of us do with delight. The Bible reminds us that the flaming sword *"turned every direction to guard the way to the tree of life"* (Genesis 3:24 NASB). Extraordinary, is it not? God is making it clear that there would be no compromise. How terrifying to be shut out from God's presence. One can only imagine the regret Adam and Eve must have felt as they stood outside the garden. Would they be shut out forever?

In the midsummer of 2007, I was forced to evacuate from my golf-side condo near San Diego. The summer heat, with temperatures nearing triple digits, scorched the mountainsides that grace the topography of my favorite city. A few years earlier (2003), I remained fast asleep through the morning fires while my neighbors had gone to safety. Somehow I managed to sleep through vigorous knocks on my door. I had just moved into the area, was still unpacking my goods, and was physically exhausted. I did not wait for a knock this time. As the fires scaled the hills around me, it was clear that I had to leave. The thick smoke made it difficult to breathe, and a gut-level fear swept over me.

Picking up my best books, passport, guitar, and a few personal items, I was in my car and saying goodbye to a coming hell. It was bumper-to-bumper traffic that day, all the way to Hotel Circle Drive, as frantic citizens fled to safety. It was a time of confusion and chaos. I settled that night on the sixth floor of a San Diego hotel, glued to the news and bracing for the worst. Restlessness began to set in after the third day.

Five days in, I decided to try to check out the damage to my home. Many news reports were warning residents not to return until it was safe to do so, but I also heard about people returning to their homes. I was only three miles away when I noticed a convoy of military vehicles barricading the streets along with soldiers armed with AK-47 rifles. That was not the scene I was hoping for. Vehicles were parked all along the road with residents standing around, on the edge of mental breakdown, as the soldiers' barricades prevented them from going home. I knew this was not for me; I turned around and headed back to my hotel.

The local news reported later that day of physical clashes between the soldiers and residents. People were willing to risk their lives to reclaim their belongings. We're human; we let nothing stand in our way. God knew that Adam, like my anarchist neighbors and me, would stop at nothing to demand our comforts. That is the true condition of the human race. Thanks are in order to Adam for that long tradition of sinful rebellion! Would Adam do whatever it took to re-enter God's presence? None of us can escape the suspicion that God's cherubim were standing guard against that very impulse.

When I truly scrutinize my own heart, I know something about mine that you also know about yours. My heart is twisted in so many ways and in so many places that I need to be re-created every day. I find a tendency in myself to want what God has clearly forbidden. The things that bring God glory are often not the things I seek. And when I do bring Him glory, I am acutely aware that I did not do it alone. Like Paul, I concede that there is *nothing good in me*—any good I do comes from the Creator. Adam had to face that realization. He had to be re-created and renewed or remain in his state of chaos.

Adam lived for 930 years (Genesis 5:5) before he died. The Bible tells us little about him after being driven out of the garden. Adam lived his remaining days outside of Eden, where he had other sons and daughters, *"in his own likeness, after his image"* (Genesis 5:3 ESV). When we first met him (Genesis 1:27), Adam bore *the moral image of God*. The moment he sinned, however, Adam could no longer reflect the moral image of His Creator. It could no longer be said that he looked like his Father. A new likeness had emerged, and a man crafted for immortal glory would now return to the dust of earth. His curious day in Eden left a trail of shattered pieces—God's masterpiece had lost its immortal beauty.

NEW CREATIONS

People tell me that I look like my father. Isn't it strange that no matter where we hide, we cannot hide from genetics? My father was a reticent man in my youth. I never really knew him, at least not in the way I needed too. I now understand that he never really had a father either, and I had to come to a place of gratitude that at least I have a father. We still have a lot of work to do, but it is ongoing. When I travel to my home country of Dominica, I spend time with him in a desperate effort to hear more bits and pieces of his story. My father does not talk about internal stuff. I asked him once about his life decisions and got a somewhat clichéd answer—the man just won't open up.

Yet for all the ways we are different, I am still struck by the fact that I am my father's son. He is a gifted painter and musician. Ever the artist, he thrives on showmanship. The man can do just about anything except have an open conversation. Those who know me best would say I am open, musical, linear, and gifted, and I strive to honor God to the best of my ability most days.

While I look like my father and possess a few of his gifts, I find that I act like my mother. She was generous and kind, and she would discuss anything and everything with me. It is in her story that I can find myself. I only wish she were around to hear and read these words. My mother, who I lost in 2008, would be proud and touched as always.

At the age of seventeen, I began to take on another likeness—that of my heavenly Father. In the year I became a Christian, although I did not realize it then, I no longer lived in the shadow of my biological father. I had been re-created and reborn to resemble my Father in heaven.

I share that likeness with all who accept the gift of God's Son. We are an army of billions, 2.1 billion and growing. We've come through the same fire, have been washed in the same blood, and are experiencing the same new life. We have the same big brother, Jesus, and we await the same promise of glory. Although we still carry the nature of Adam, we've been re-created and made acceptable for union with our Creator. Access is granted to all of us through the blood of Jesus. But Paul reminds us to: *"Put on the new self, created after the likeness of God in true righteousness and holiness"* (Ephesians 4:24 esv).

The best of us don't have it together, and we admit it openly. We follow in the steps of brothers and sisters like Abraham, Moses, David, the woman at the well,

Solomon, Rehab, and Paul. Among them are liars, adulterers, cowards, womanizers, and persecutors. The Spirit who told their stories did not hide their failures, and neither should we. Their greatness was not determined by their own actions but the actions of God who called, re-created, and loved them, even in the midst of their sin. None of these men or women could boast or take credit for their restoration.

Abraham's name was changed from Abram, meaning "high father," to Abraham, which means "father of a multitude." Moses' name meant "Savior," and although he began with resistance, he did ultimately live up to his name. David's name means "friend," and he was called "a man after God's own heart." Solomon's name comes from the same Hebrew root as *shalom*, which means "peace." Paul's name was unique—it means "little." Had he lived in our time, he might have been dubbed "Shorty" or something worse. Tradition tells us that he was bow-legged and bald. How ironic that the man they called "Little" became the greatest apostle of the Christian faith, penning thirteen of the books of the New Testament!

God likes to rearrange things, and according to the Apostle John, He will do it again: *"I will make him a pillar in the temple of my God. Never shall he go out of it, and I will write on him the name of my God, and the name of the city of my God, the new Jerusalem, which comes down from my God out of heaven, and my own new name. He who has an ear, let him hear what the Spirit says to the churches"* (Revelation 3:12–13 ESV).

Can you hear your name? God is calling each of us to be a new creation, the likes of which we've never known. He is casting off the old self and making something new. Our names, even from birth, were marred by sin and covered in debris. He is making us over again, in His image.

Yes, our sins are gone! Abraham, the liar, was called a friend of God. David, the adulterer, was the only man designated "the one after God's own heart." Paul, the murderer, had more revelations than anyone before or since. These men and others like them did not earn or bribe their way into God's favor. They all received it freely because of love—a love that looks past yesterday's failures. Like them, our names are written in red. God has a special name for each of us, one that only He knows. Like them, our destinies are certain and strong, built on a new foundation and decorated with blessings. They are not earned through self-righteousness, but they are won for us by Christ, the Second Adam.

For all of the scandals, failures, and pathetic choices we make, it's hard sometimes to realize that God's love for us is actually real. So often, we return to the field of debris that does not exist in the mind and sight of God. We tease ourselves with lies, thinking ourselves worthy of judgment, not grace. Yet, while it's true that we are unworthy in ourselves, we have been made acceptable to God, qualified and worthy to eat of the Tree of Life. The gates are opened to us, thanks to Jesus, and the flaming sword cannot hurt us. But we must realize that it's not on our own merit but on His that we enter. God reminds us through Peter that we've been re-created by God to manifest His glory: *"But you are a chosen race, a royal priesthood, a holy nation, a people for his own possession, that you may proclaim the excellencies of him who called you out of darkness into his marvelous light"* (1 Peter 2:9 ESV). We have been made new. Old things are gone; a new day has come for us!

"London businessman Lindsay Clegg told the story of a warehouse property he was selling. The building had been empty for months and needed repairs. Vandals had damaged the doors, smashed the windows, and strewn trash around the interior. As he showed a prospective buyer the property, Clegg took pains to say that he would replace the broken windows, bring in a crew to correct any structural damage, and clean out the garbage. 'Forget about the repairs,' the buyer said. 'When I buy this place, I'm going to build something completely different. I don't want the building; I want the site.'"[19] That's what God wants to do with us.

Compared with the renovation God has in mind, our efforts to improve our own lives are as trivial as sweeping a warehouse slated for the wrecking ball. When we become God's, the old life is over (2 Corinthians 5:17). He makes all things new. What God wants is the site and the permission to rebuild. No matter how messed up we feel, God wants to make us new, not partly but fully new. He offers us a new image, a new hope, a new name, and a new home. This begins the moment we open the book of our heart to his eyes.

VISIONS OF PARADISE

Eden was a place of beauty. Rivers, trees, and a luscious made up its rolling landscape. These all provided Adam and Eve an open door to fellowship and communion with God. It was where heaven touched earth and where man touched God. In that sense, Eden was nothing more than a vision or preview of the paradise of heaven. Because of sin, however, this true paradise of God was taken back to heaven—not the physical location but the presence of God Himself, which made it paradise. In what follows, you will discover that Eden is returning for a second act, with a new keeper.

God was in the midst of the garden, giving it liveliness and meaning. It was Eden only when God was in it, and when He departed, it became just another garden without the magic it once had. Take the temple, for example. When Solomon built and later inaugurated the temple in Jerusalem, God marked its significance by entering in a blaze of glory. It was the temple because the holy God had entered to make His presence felt. But when God departed the temple (1 Samuel 4:21), emptiness crept in announcing *Ichabod,* for the glory had departed. And this is also true of people, for the Bible tells us: *"The Spirit of the LORD departed from Saul"* (1 Samuel 16:14 ESV). The same end befell Samson: *"He did not know that the LORD had left him"* (Judges 16:20 ESV). Both the temple and these individuals became empty spaces without God's presence. So it was in Eden after sin entered. God, by His absence, brought Eden out of earth back into heaven where it originated.

How do we know this? First is the fact that Satan was in Eden before its geographical location on earth: *"You were in Eden, the garden of God; every precious stone was your covering: the ruby, the topaz and the diamond; the beryl, the onyx and the jasper; the lapis lazuli, the turquoise and the emerald; and the gold, the workmanship of your settings and sockets, was in you. On the day that you were created they were prepared"* (Ezekiel 28:13 NASB). So Satan was in Eden before the Fall.

We saw in Genesis a river similar to that of heaven. Genesis 2:10 tells us: *"A river flowed out to Eden to water the garden, and there it divided and became four rivers"* (ESV). In the last book of the Bible, the Apostle John, while in exile on the Isle of Patmos, revealed a happy vision of our storied ending. In it is a river with a striking similarity to the Garden of Eden: *"Then the angel showed me the river of the water of life, bright as crystal, flowing from the throne of God and of the Lamb through the middle of the street of the city; also, on either side of the river, the tree of life with its twelve kinds of fruit, yielding its fruit each month. The leaves of the tree were for the healing of the nations"* (Revelation 22:1–2 ESV). This is Eden again, offering man a new beginning in the perfect presence of his Maker.

Like the river in Eden, this river flows out from its infinite source, pouring into the Tree of Life, yielding twelve kinds of fruit and having leaves that bring healing to the nations. It is interesting that the fruit of the Garden of Eden brought death, whereas this garden brings life. The Tree of Life in Eden was guarded with a flaming sword, but this garden is open to the nations, bringing healing. How thrilling to know that we are welcomed back to the true Eden, to enter God's garden after what Adam and Eve did so long ago! This news is for all of us, the wounded children of Adam who have suffered outside the garden, toiling through thorns and thistles in the scorching heat of sin. Our wait is over, and our time has come to join our Maker and enter in.

I can almost feel and even touch this moment as it sinks in. Nothing will fill our hearts more than coming home at the end of our labors and finally be free. Those who turned in faith to Jesus will not be forgotten when God opens Eden again. With tickets in hand, we will enter. *"To the one who is victorious, I will give the right to eat from the tree of life, which is in the paradise of God"* (Revelation 2:7 NIV). This paradise or enclosed garden will be home to all of us who endured with patience. We, the redeemed sons and daughters of Adam, will lift our voices in the company of cherubim without swords. We will be singing about the redeeming love of God and enjoying the fruits of God's bounty in the glory of Jesus forever and ever.

ARRIVING

Life is like a high sea drama with danger, fear, and uncertainty gripping our hearts. But all of this will give way to a new day. We will realize that our trials on earth could not compare to the glory to be revealed to us. Our eyes will behold our Maker as we look with awesome wonder at what has been kept for us and will be revealed before our eyes. We will enter and be thrilled at the magnificent wonders of Heaven.

As we stand at the edge of eternity and take our first steps through the gates of the eternal city, we will pause to remember our journey. As we stand there, we will remember how our curious nature led us down a path of danger, skewing our vision, marring our image, destroying our innocence, and forcing us out of paradise. We will remember Satan's lies and false promises that led us to abandon our post, ignore our limits, and forget our place. Likewise, we will reflect upon the desert of sin that left our hearts parched and thirsty for living water. Then we will recall the vices of hate, anger, jealousy, and pride that led to the massacre of our brothers, corrupted our sense of respect for one another, and plundered our sacred dreams.

I believe we will remember our wasted years in retreat from God's perfect laws that were meant to revive us, make us wise, give us joy, and bring us enlightenment. Foolishly, we forgot our common humanity through the great injustice of racism that divided our loyalties and caused us to veer from our destiny. We will remember that we were neutralized through isolation, family wounds, and legalism, as the war within was lost and our hearts made for God were laid to waste. But that was not the end to our trouble. We will remember how sin stole our innocence.

But we will be suddenly interrupted, as a father interrupts his apologetic son or daughter. He will remind us of what happened before sunrise. He will take us, the sons and daughters of Adam, by the hand. In that moment, we will forget all of yesterday's trials and sins. Our starts and false starts will not be found, and neither will our regrets or tears, for He will, in one gesture, *"Wipe every tear from [our] eyes"* (Revelation 21:4 NKJV). Then, with no burdens to carry, no grudges to hold, and no fear to endure, we will enter into the glory of God and see our Father and the Holy Spirit standing beside the Son with a multitude of angels welcoming us to our new paradise! No language will be adequate to describe what we will experience. So we will turn, fall on our knees, and raise our faces to the Son.

Imagine. There you are. There I am, at home, with thousands upon thousands of angels in joyful assembly with the church of the firstborn. There is no more sorrow, sadness, or mourning—our faith has become sight. There is no more night, for the Son lights everything in this new eternal city. It is here that you must join me and see with your own eyes, touch with your own hands, hear with your own ears, and believe with your own heart. Then you too will know fully what was meant by the Apostle Paul when he told us: *"No eye has seen, no ear has heard, and no mind has imagined what God has prepared for those who love him"* (1 Corinthians 2:9 NLT).

I am so awestruck that my words fail me. Here, in this place, my tongue is tied. Are yours too? Just then, the words of an angel ring out, as if to narrate what I was beholding: "*The city does not need the sun or the moon to shine on it, for the glory of God gives it light, and the Lamb is its lamp. The nations will walk by its light, and the kings of the earth will bring their splendor into it. On no day will its gates ever be shut, for there will be no night there. The glory and honor of the nations will be brought into it. Nothing impure will ever enter it, nor will anyone who does what is shameful or deceitful, but only those whose names are written in the Lamb's book of life*" (Revelation 21:23–27 NIV). I stand there wide-eyed and amazed!

"*Then the angel showed me the river of the water of life, as clear as crystal, flowing from the throne of God and of the Lamb down the middle of the great street of the city. On each side of the river stood the tree of life, bearing twelve crops of fruit, yielding its fruit every month. And the leaves of the tree are for the healing of the nations. No longer will there be any curse*" (Revelation 22:1–3 NIV). "Ah," I said the moment I heard this, "this is Eden, the garden of heaven." Now we will dwell with our Maker as it was in the beginning. We can walk with Him in the cool of the day with our image restored—the curse will be over. Man will now rule again as it was meant to be. We will live in perfect obedience, perfect innocence, perfect love, perfect satisfaction, and perfect glory, and we will live a perfect life.

But wait. If all this is true of us, must we not reimagine who we are? Can we go on living casual lives when God makes so much of us? He has fitted us for something amazing. That which was broken has been renewed. Your life story has a new ending. We have been remade and reshaped into His image. Brokenness is only our past, not our future. Earth left us marred, but God has dreamed up bigger things for us. So what are we waiting for? When will we begin to live up to God's dreams for us? The way we live each day is our response: Do we embrace our future glory, or live in the dust of earth? Heaven calls out. Glory waits.

Notes

1. Gordon Talbot, *A Study of the Book of Genesis* (Harrisburg: Christian Publications, Inc., 1981), 21.
2. C. F. Keil and F. Delitzsch, *Commentary on the Old Testament* (Peabody: Hendrickson Pub, Inc., 2006), 53.
3. Saint Augustine, *Confessions*, translated by Garry Willis (London: Penguin Books Ltd., 2002), 7.
4. Jacob Needleman, *Why Can't We Be Good?* (New York: Penguin Books Ltd., 2007), 140.
5. John Piper, *Future Grace* (Oregon: Multnomah Books, 1995), 9.
6. C.S. Lewis, *Mere Christianity* (San Francisco: Harper Collins, 2001), 137.
7. Blaise Pascal, *Pensées*, translated by A.J. Krailsheimer (New York: Penguin Books, 1995), 150.
8. Eric Metaxas, *Bonhoeffer: Pastor, Martyr, Prophet, Spy* (Nashville: Thomas Nelson Publishers 2010), 606.
9. Blaise Pascal, *Pensées*, op. cit., 127.
10. Dictionary.com
11. J. Philippe Rushton, Robin J. H. Russell, and Pamela A. Wells, *Genetic Similarity Theory: Beyond Kin Selection* (Plenum Publishing Corporation, 1984), 179.

12. Marcus Aurelius, *Meditations* (New York: Everyman's Library, 1946), 40.
13. Agatha Christie, *An Autobiography* (London: Harper Collins, 1977), 93.
14. Natalie Babbitt, *Tuck Everlasting* (New York: Farrar, Straus & Girouz, 1975), 45.
15. *Merriam-Webster* Dictionary.
16. Martin Luther, "A Mighty Fortress Is Our God."
17. Doug Goins, *The Victory Over Death* (Discovery Publishing, 199), a sermon, Catalog No. 4539.
18. Matthew Henry, *Commentary on the Whole Bible* (Nashville: Thomas Nelson, 1997), 9.
19. Ian L. Wilson, source unknown.

Milton Keynes UK
Ingram Content Group UK Ltd.
UKHW012253291123
433483UK00006B/375